526

Taken
by
the
Muse

ANNE WHEELER

Taken by the Muse

NeWest Press

Copyright © Anne Wheeler 2020

All rights reserved. The use of any part of this publication — reproduced, transmitted in any form or by any means, electronic, mechanical, recording or otherwise, or stored in a retrieval system — without the prior consent of the publisher is an infringement of the copyright law. In the case of photocopying or other reprographic copying of the material, a licence must be obtained from Access Copyright before proceeding.

Library and Archives Canada Cataloguing in Publication
Title: Taken by the muse : on the path to becoming a filmmaker / Anne Wheeler.
Names: Wheeler, Anne, author.
Identifiers: Canadiana (print) 20200189158 | Canadiana (ebook) 20200189425
ISBN 9781774390016 (softcover) | ISBN 9781774390023 (EPUB) |
ISBN 9781774390030 (Kindle)
Subjects: LCSH: Wheeler, Anne, | LCSH: Women motion picture producers and directors — Canada — Biography. | LCSH: Women television producers and directors — Canada — Biography. | LCSH: Motion picture producers and directors — Canada — Biography. | LCSH: Television producers and directors — Canada — Biography. | LCGFT: Autobiographies.
Classification: LCC PN1998.3.W44 A3 2020 | DDC 791.43092 — DC23

Board editor: Eva Radford
Book design: Natalie Olsen, Kisscut Design
Cover images: © jumpingsack/shutterstock.com, drawbot/shutterstock.com
Author photo: Rosamond Norbury

EARLY MORNIN' RAIN
Words and Music by GORDON LIGHTFOOT
© 1965 (Renewed) WC MUSIC CORP.
All Rights Reserved
Used By Permission of ALFRED MUSIC

NeWest Press acknowledges the Canada Council for the Arts, the Alberta Foundation for the Arts, and the Edmonton Arts Council for support of our publishing program. This project is funded in part by the Government of Canada. ¶ NeWest Press acknowledges that the land on which we operate is Treaty 6 territory and a traditional meeting ground and home for many Indigenous Peoples, including Cree, Saulteaux, Niitsitapi (Blackfoot), Métis, and Nakota Sioux.

#201, 8540–109 Street   Edmonton, Alberta   T6G 1E6
780.432.9427
NeWest Press   www.newestpress.com

No bison were harmed in the making of this book.
Printed and bound in Canada   3 4 5   22 21 20

To my Grandmothers,
Rose Lee Morrill Wheeler
and
Carrie Hill Edwards Pawsey

CONTENTS

FILMWEST OFFICES, 1972. ANNE WHEELER ARCHIVES.

INTRODUCTION

Edmonton, December 1986

I WOKE UP in the middle of the night with a sense of urgency and a song my mother often played ringing in my head. "Don't give me posies, when it's shoesies that I need!"

Knowing sleep would be impossible, I pulled on my parka, stepped into my winter boots, and trudged across the backyard through the deep snow, to my writing shack. The door was iced up, frozen shut, so it took a good strong yank to break it open.

It had been weeks since I'd written anything. With two young sons to raise and a small film company to run, it had been hard to get beyond the practical tasks of each day. I needed these times of silence, of aloneness; I needed the mental space to be creative. Tonight, perhaps, the magic would spill out of me.

I turned on my spanking new Columbia computer and opened up the file for *Bye Bye Blues*. It seemed like I had been grinding away for years on this epic screenplay inspired by my mother's wartime years. I had already written six or eight drafts. Maybe more, I'd lost count. They were all so mediocre — just scratching the surface and revealing nothing of substance.

There I was, starting all over again at 2 a.m., shivering in the dim light, staring at the computer screen as it flickered into life.

"Come on baby, I know it's cold in here, but let's give this one last try."

Suddenly the phone rang. Who on earth could that be?

Thinking it had to be a wrong number, I answered with a curt "Hello," ready to cut the caller off quickly.

There was a slight pause at the other end, then a smoky tone. "Is this Anne Wheeler?"

I could not place the voice — it could be anyone. My name was in the phone book; my number was no secret. At this hour, it had to be a wrong number or someone weird.

"Yes, it is," I stated flatly, offering no encouragement. "Who is this?"

"I'm sorry, did I wake you up?"

"Not exactly, no. But who are you? It's an odd hour to be calling."

"It's Margaret Laurence."

"Oh my God," I blurted. "I didn't think I'd ever hear from you!"

Margaret Laurence was my all-time favourite writer — and a literary giant! She was a three-time winner of the Governor General's award; anyone who had taken high school English had studied her work.

Two years ago, I'd had the privilege of adapting one of her short stories to film. *To Set Our House in Order* was semi-autobiographical; it was told in the first person by Vanessa MacLeod, who, like Margaret, grew up in a small prairie town and eventually left to become a writer. I accepted the assignment to write and direct the film with trepidation. How could I live up to Margaret's genius and reputation — especially when I knew that the book was essentially about her?

And this was a particularly difficult story to adapt. It traces the inner thoughts of Vanessa at the age of ten, when she and her family moved into her paternal grandmother's home. Miserably, she witnessed how Ewen, her father, a doctor, whom she'd always idolized, was repeatedly humiliated by his own mother. With time, she learns that her father as a young man went off to war with his younger brother, but came back alone. His mother blames him for the loss. There was nothing he could do to win her forgiveness.

I didn't want to use a narrative voice-over, which I could have lifted from the book. Instead, I wanted to create some situations that would illuminate the girl's insights. I asked the producers if I could please talk to Ms. Laurence so I could share my ideas with her before I began to write. They reported back that she did not want to talk to me, that I should go ahead and do my job. This was an unsettling response. After struggling through several drafts, fraught with self-doubt, I submitted a script with my innovations.

Again, I asked if I could talk to the author once she had read my screenplay. I had taken considerable licence and wanted to be sure it did not trouble her. I wanted to get it right. I wanted her approval. But again, she was absolutely clear: She had no desire to read the script. She didn't want to see a work in progress; she wanted to see the film once it was finished.

So I had no choice. We shot the film as I had written.

The little movie was finished with great care and a VHS tape was sent to Ms. Laurence immediately.

There was no response.

I thought perhaps she would watch it when it aired on CBC television and send me a message, any message, good or bad. The reviews were complimentary, the audience substantial, and, even though it was a short film, it garnered a few awards.

But I never heard from her.

Until now.

Here she is on the phone, more than a year since we sent her the package. I am choked up and can hardly think of what to say.

"Well, ah ... it's good to hear from you."

"Yes, well, one of the producers gave me this phone number some time ago now. I'm glad it's still yours! What time is it there?"

"Two something, but no problem. I'm up writing, kind of. Trying. My kids and husband are all sleeping."

"Good for you. How many kids do you have?"

"Two. Boys. Twins."

"Well, that was expedient of you!" Her chuckle is low and friendly.

"Yes, I got lucky I guess. It's after 4 a.m. your time isn't it?"

"Yes, I don't sleep much."

"Ah. We have that in common. I'm a night owl for sure."

There is a pause, and I am ready for anything. If she didn't like it, I will take it like a big girl and absorb the disappointment. Maybe I'll learn something.

"So, I don't watch much TV," she confesses. "Actually, I don't have one, and I don't have a video player either, but a friend brought one over last night and we watched the movie together."

"Good, good," I manage to squeak out. My throat has gone tight.

"Well. I loved it. I thought it was so good."

"You did?" Oh wow, I think I'm going to cry.

"Yes! I couldn't imagine how you would reveal the moment, the revelation, you know, that takes place inside her head — there's not much to see, physically, in the book. But you created the perfect situation. It moved me to tears."

"Oh my God, I'm so relieved! I veered so far from what you wrote — in order to say what I believed you were saying!"

"That's it! That's why I loved it. You understood my intention. You said it through the images and the performances. You didn't need a damn voice telling the audience what Vanessa was thinking and feeling. When she goes looking for her father and finds him, alone, weeping like a child, and then she puts her arms around him, like a mother ... that really undid me. It said it all."

I don't know what to say. I blurt, "The actors were terrific, weren't they?"

"Yes, yes. Perfect. I felt I knew them all. I did know them all! I was so relieved, I wanted to phone and tell you."

"Thank you ... so much." I sit for a moment and absorb the affirmation. How many times had I beaten myself up, thinking I hadn't upheld the integrity of her work?

I hear a familiar tinkle of sound, a glass perhaps. It nudges me.

"Are you drinking Scotch right now?" I venture.

"Yes, in fact. I have a single malt open, right here. Just about to pour myself another."

"Would you mind if I run into my house and get mine? I think we should have a drink together."

She laughs. "That's a damn good idea. Go get it!"

Warmed by the Scotch, we had a long and lingering

talk. She explained that she had not participated in the film because she did not want to hinder me with her involvement. She didn't want me second-guessing her preferences while finding my own way to the heart of the story. She had come to know that, in order for an artist to do her best, whether she is a writer, singer, filmmaker, or whatever, she must feel free to explore for herself and then make choices based on her own instincts and wisdom. There are a million "right ways" and she wanted me to choose what was right for me.

"Thank you for giving me the liberty."

"Thank you for taking such care with my words."

We came to realize that we had much in common: our pioneering grandparents; our lives having been defined by the loss of our fathers; our travels, motherhood, the loneliness of writing, and the paralysis of self-doubt. She told me stories of her youth, of the people she had met and known who had encouraged her to become a writer.

"What about you?" she asked. "I was told that you made an extraordinary documentary about your doctor father who was a prisoner of the Japanese."

"Yes. Making it was a very humbling experience; I didn't really know him, you see. He didn't talk about it, ever. I discovered he was 'God-like' to his patients in that camp."

"He died young?"

"Yes ... like yours ... I often wonder what I might be doing if he were still alive."

"He'd be proud of you, I suspect."

"Not so sure. I remember once telling him I wanted to be an actor and he was decidedly against it."

"Typical of his generation. Wanting the best for you, I'm sure."

"Yes, I understand that now. He knew his life would be cut short because of his war experience; he wanted me to have something to fall back on in case I married badly or was widowed."

"And still, here you are ... a writer, an artist, and making a good living." We both chuckle.

"Yes. He would be surprised. And I took a most circuitous route."

"Ah yes. Most of us do. It's pretty much necessary. If you hope to have any kind of impact — you must be capable of understanding the reality of others, to see a situation from a place other than your own. And now you are writing about your mother?"

"Yes, and I'm stymied."

"Well, writing about those we love is always the most difficult and the most fulfilling."

"I feel shackled by a need to protect her and the rest of my family. I don't want to hurt or offend anyone."

"Yes, I understand. My advice is: don't look at their lives from the outside. You need to get inside their very being. If you can do that, you will share their sense of discovery, their most intimate moments; and the revelations that unfold will drive you forward."

"With my mom's story, I am trying to fill in the private spaces, to reveal what she was experiencing internally. Thing is, I don't know what she thought. She can tell me what she did ... but not what she felt. She's always kept that to herself. I don't want to interrogate her."

"What you know — for sure — is not enough," she states, matter-of-factly. "It is never enough! You have to take the risk and go far beyond what you know!"

"That's it, exactly! That is the crux of my dilemma! What I know is not enough! I will never know what my mother really believed, or said, or regretted!"

"No ... but you can use her actions along with your own intuition. Try not to censor yourself. What is revealed on the outside is rarely close to what is happening on the inside. You have to put yourself in her position — be her. Live her situation, her circumstances. Your curiosity and imagination will take it from there. Do for yourself what you did with my story. Eventually you will understand why she made the decisions she made."

"What about the truth?"

"The truth! The real truth?"

"Yes."

"You'll never find out the real truth from her — even if she tells you as much as she can remember. You have to discover your own truth."

After we hung up, I sat there in the dark, feeling utterly amazed. How providential that she had phoned this number, my office number, at this hour — and I was here! It was a call I could have easily missed — it felt like some strange force had been at work. No one else could have mentored better me than Margaret Laurence. No one else could have related so closely to my task; no one else could have stepped in with such wisdom.

Now, thirty-plus years later, I feel it's my time to pass some insights, and it is her voice that guides me. I have written screenplays and the occasional song, but never prose. It is a totally different medium, and I feel she is here with me as I step onto what was her platform. The advice she gave me years ago still rings true as I contemplate what it is I want to share with you.

This collection recounts a series of serendipitous encounters I had on my way to becoming a filmmaker. Such a career was not on the list of what a woman could be in the sixties. There was no film school or #metoo movement to suggest that my talent was worthy of attention; that it could provide a viable living; that I could be a visual artist, a writer, or a performer of any kind and not be a burden and a disappointment to my widowed mother. To follow my fancy would have been seen as a selfish thing to do.

But my passion was repeatedly stirred by unexpected challenges, by people who saw me more clearly than I saw myself. It was when I took risks, or remained open to possibilities, listened to my own rhythm, that my muse would suddenly be there and alter my course. It was not always through a person, though when it was it was never someone I would have expected. There were times when my muse was invisibly at work, provoking me, setting up obstacles, surprising me, triggering some magic, seducing me with the possibility that I could live with purpose, doing something I loved.

So now I aspire to be a conduit for your muse. Like Margaret.

But where do I begin?

Like many of my childhood pals, I followed a well-worn path into my twenties. After completing a bachelor's degree in mathematics, I travelled Europe as a way of finishing my education. But I wasn't "finished." I was restless and wary of settling down. I confronted my discontent with youthful abandon. After a year of teaching music at a junior high school, I quit and took off to circle the globe.

Without a strong sense of purpose, I became a wanderer. In a way, I was lost. I was at my lowest when destiny intervened and my circuitous journey of self-discovery truly began.

These are stories I have shared with friends, students, colleagues, and other raconteurs. In the telling, they have become richer, more intricate, and decidedly more playful. They all take place in the seventies — a decade of unprecedented freedom and privilege.

I have written them in the present tense, which means I have used the terms and expressions of the day with no intention to offend. For instance, in the seventies, in my world we still used the word Indian to define a huge population that included First Nations, Mexicans, Métis, and Indians from India — basically anyone one who was not white was assumed to be Indian. I didn't see a black person or hear the word Muslim until I was in my late teens. All Asians were Chinese. All visible minorities had nicknames that are now inappropriate. In Edmonton, we had French and Ukrainian and the rest were pretty much unidentified. The diversity of language used today to identify people, their cultural inheritance, their sexual preference, is a measure of how the world has changed. In reaching back to know myself as a young woman, I have been mindful of how unaware I was, how ignorant and insensitive. On the other hand, it was in part my naïvety that kept me safe and optimistic about the future.

As Margaret Laurence advised, I have filled the spaces between my recollections with possibilities. While my memories of these real events hold these stories in place, I have allowed them to acquire a will of their own, determined to be more than a report of where I went and what I did. With age and experience, my stories have gathered meaning, and I have come to know myself better. I hope they will stir my readers' curiosity about themselves and the lives they are living.

A few months after her phone call, I heard that Margaret had taken her own life. She left quietly, without any fuss, only sixty-one years old. Having terminal lung cancer, she decided to save her family, friends, and herself the anguish of a slow, painful death. She must have been sick the night she called, but nonetheless wanted to take care of some unfinished business and pass on to me something of what she had learned. She was so honest and generous. I regret that I never got a chance to meet her in person, to thank her for the gift of that call. She gave me the courage to explore the world within and to find my own way out.

Anne Wheeler

SOUTH OF MOMBASA

May 1971

EVERYTHING IS GREY. The night is grey, the road is grey —
no wonder I almost collided with that elephant back there!
Coming to a screeching halt, I missed her by an inch, and she
didn't even flinch. She just stared at me with her tiny eyes, so
small that they barely kicked back the light. Slowly, calmly, she
shimmied to the side, regarding me with disdain, giving me
just enough room to drive around her. She was right. I am an
idiot to be driving at night, alone and exhausted, emotionally
unhinged, talking to myself — crossing the plains of Africa.

I should have stayed in Nairobi for the night, but the
tension between Michael and me was unbearable. I had been
in a whirl, hopelessly impulsive, throwing my stuff into my
poor wee car, leaving behind what I couldn't squeeze inside
or strap onto the roof. I should have taken her in for servicing
before I left. I didn't even send my brother a telegram, warning
him that I'd be landing on his doorstep in a couple of days —
alone. I left in such a fury, I hadn't even changed my clothes,
and now I was headed south, bound for Tanga, Tanzania.

It's hard to believe that a week ago I was working in the basement of the Nairobi National Museum with my fiancé, Michael, an ambitious, handsome Harvard archaeologist. We'd only met a few months back; our romance had been intense and exciting. I volunteered to work on his doctoral dig. He loved that I was a cowgirl, happy to camp out. I loved that he had such a passion for his work, such a keen curiosity. He spoke Swahili fluently. We got on well, the work got done, and the place he had chosen to dig was rich with artifacts. After the fieldwork was complete, I stayed on to help him sort out and log the findings. Being an old-fashioned man of action, he wrote to my widowed mother and asked for my hand in marriage. She was thrilled that I had landed a good man with a future and some sense of protocol — quite different from the guys I had been bringing home in recent years.

I knew my family was worried about me. My three older brothers were all happily married, raising children. I was the odd one out, constantly changing direction, going from one job to another, never showing up with the same man twice. Suddenly I had taken off and disappeared somewhere east of Europe. For a while, nobody knew where I was. I sent postcards from Greece, Syria, and Egypt that arrived in no particular order, with no return address. When I did resurface, engaged to Michael, it looked as though I was finally going to live a more conventional life.

I had said yes to Michael's proposal without fully anticipating the implications. It wasn't until we were on our way to get married at my brother's home in Tanga — he and his wife had agreed to be witnesses — that I realized I had made a big mistake.

Michael was waxing on about our future — how he had applied and been accepted for "married housing" at Harvard where we'd live for the next two or three years while he completed his thesis. I was going to love Boston, the States, the work, the people, his parents — and the courses I could take to better assist him. A feeling of dread overtook me as he sketched out his plan.

I couldn't let my life funnel down into his — labelling artifacts, writing up proposals, fulfilling his career. He was a great guy, ready to commit, to take care of me, to love me, to provide for me. It should have felt like a dream come true, but it didn't. Why? Why couldn't I embrace this next obvious step in my life? What did I want?

While sitting in the car beside him, on our way to our wedding, I realized that, in truth, I loved the freedom of being a loner, of taking the path uncharted. I hated being locked into a rigid plan, especially when it was someone else's. There was an undeniable need inside me to do something of meaning; I just hadn't figured out what that was.

So, even though we were on our way to tie the knot, I called off the wedding. Michael was overcome with disbelief, convinced that I didn't know my own mind. I was ashamed of myself, sick with remorse — but resolute. We pulled over to the side of the roadway and batted my decision back and forth, whacking it to death — until finally he was convinced that I was not going to change my mind. We turned around and drove back to Nairobi in silence.

That was yesterday. Now I am rudderless and heading into the unknown. No woman in my family has ever remained single. Education was always considered to be a "fall back" luxury. But, like the Bob Dylan song, "The Times They Are a-Changin'."

Before I met Michael, my plan was to stop in Kenya, work for six months, and then travel on to South Africa where I would take a boat to India via the Seychelles. Now I'm broke, with nothing to my name but this beat-up Volkswagen, jam-packed with African drums, bolts of brightly printed cloth, Makonde carvings, salad bowls, baskets within baskets, and a bag of film I can't afford to develop.

I was going to stop in Mombasa, get myself organized, make a plan, and get some sleep, but I got turned around in the tiny streets and ended up in a slum near the old port — a place of poverty beyond all imagining. I was hoping to find a cheap hotel with secure parking. No such place existed. Luckily, some friendly teenagers hanging out at a gas station led me to the Likoni Ferry, which took me over to the south side of the city where there were several modest motels on the main road out of town. But these places also seemed too dicey; the lock on my driver's door was broken, so I'd have to haul everything inside my room and find someone to stand guard over my car all night. Too tired to contemplate such a task, I decided to keep on driving.

Gawd, I love my car. It's so much easier having my own wheels. I travelled through Europe by train, around the Mediterranean by freighter, through the Middle East by bus, down the Nile by barge, and by every means possible across Sudan and Ethiopia. It took me six months to get from London to Kenya. Travelling alone, I sometimes felt like I was up for grabs. A couple of times, I almost got claimed, like a stray cow, by men who thought they'd add me to their herd.

I bought my vw Beetle when I first arrived in Nairobi — it's become my place of refuge and my suitcase on wheels.

Consequently, I have accumulated a market-load of stuff — more than I would ever be able to carry. East Africa has gone through a political shift in the past few months. The borders between Uganda, Tanzania, and Kenya, which were open when I arrived, are now heavily secured. The three countries no longer share the same currency, or a sense of "oneness." The volleying for power has made everyone nervous. In fact, there are no other cars on the road. There is a tiny border crossing coming up, between Kenya and Tanzania, and I'm afraid that my passport, which reveals all of my wanderings and backtracking, will provoke a lot of questions.

As I drive up to the booth, it looks like the gate has been closed for the night. I might have to wait until dawn for someone to show up, so I cut the engine and start to make myself comfortable. Mysteriously, the gate opens on its own, as though I should just pass through and carry on, but I know better than to cross a border without getting a visa stamp.

"Hello," I call out, "anyone here?"

A head pops up from beneath the small window in the booth and two tired eyes squint out at me. I swear the border guard thinks I'm an illusion as he comes out of his box, carrying his gun, and straightening his uniform. Wiping off his sleepy face, he marches right up to my window and takes a closer look — right down my low-cut top. I realize I'm dressed inappropriately.

"Jambo!" I smile, using my limited Swahili vocabulary, leaning forward, blocking his view of my cleavage. He responds, asking me a question I don't understand. He's maybe forty, heavy-set, his uniform stretched across his ample belly.

Holding out my passport, I continue with a phrase I have

memorized. "Ninahitajipasipotiyanguiliyopigwa, bwana. Ni muhimusana." (I need my passport stamped, sir. It's important.) "Muhimusana." Agreeing that it is important, he chuckles, amused by my pronunciation. He looks inside the car, curious. "You one person, mwali (young woman)?"

I know I look young to him; Africans often guess me to be a teenager, even though I'm twenty-four. "Ni nzuri!" (It's all good!) My "go to" response to almost everything.

"Ni nzurisana!" (Not all good!) He then talks on, gesturing. I pick out the words "barabara" (road) and "mbaya" (bad).

Is he is suggesting that I should stay here until morning? I keep a smile on my face and remain still. He leafs through my passport, toying with me, I think. "Unanjaa?" he asks. (Are you hungry?)

This, I understand. "No, asante." (No, thank you.)

He asks me something more, still smiling. I think he has just offered me a bed. I remain reserved, acutely aware that we are totally alone.

"Wewenimwemasana." (You are very kind.) It's a phrase I've learned for situations such as this.

That's it. That's all the Swahili I know.

He nods and then mutters something to himself. Handing my passport back, he touches my hand just a little too long. Then he motions for me to follow him through the gate.

I note that he has no vehicle here other than a pedal bike. I stuff my papers back into my pouch and drive slowly beside him. He points to a place to park, underneath an old baobab tree, beside a shed. I gradually speed up, and when I think I have enough distance from him, I take off. Pedal to the metal, smooth tires spinning, dust kicking up, I get back on the roadway and bounce off into the darkness.

In my rear-view mirror, I see him waving at me to come back, holding up his gun. We both know he cannot catch me and there isn't time to take a shot. I feel guilty — I could not find my trust. He might have been a kind man, being protective, and now I have slighted him. The truth is that my nerves are frayed, and I would not have slept for a moment.

Beyond the border, the highway becomes a narrow sandy road, cutting through the palm forest that crimps the shore of the Indian Ocean. I've been warned that at night, truck drivers, often drunk and tired, own this road, driving at breakneck speeds with their headlights off. My own headlights are dim and my windshield is webbed with multiple fractures. I drive with my windows down so I will hear an approaching truck over the roar of my noisy engine in time to pull off the road.

My little car, affectionately called Dudu ("Bug") has taken me all over East Africa and into the Congo. I have run of gas a couple of times, but it has never let me down.

Until now.

With only the shadowy palm trees as my witnesses, the sound of my motor crescendos with a series of raucous vibrations and a final loud CRACK! The lights expire as Dudu seizes up and dies.

Rolling to a halt, I sit, listening to the night sounds of the forest — the hum of insects, the wind in the trees, some faraway voices — and then — oh no!

I hear a horn in the distance and the distinctive rumble of an 18-wheeler! I pound on my horn and something explodes with a bang. What was that!? A gun?

Doesn't matter! I gotta get this car off the road right now!

Jumping out, I push against the doorframe. The car starts to move, but as soon as I turn the wheel, it comes to a stop. The tires are wedged into the sandy ruts; I don't have the strength to push Dudu over the higher centre of the road. Wailing with the effort, I rock it back and forth, again and again. Wet with sweat and fear, I hear the truck honking, getting closer. Maybe if I get my stuff out of the car, it will be lighter and more manageable.

Like a madwoman, I throw clothes, drums, carvings, camera, salad bowls, baskets, as much as I can grab, into the blackness. Again, I try to move the car off the road, but I'm hopelessly stuck now. I am ready to run down the road toward the truck with the wild hope of stopping the driver, when I hear a babble of voices.

Turning, I see a cluster of torches marching toward me through the palms. A dozen or more men emerge from the shadows. A couple of them are running down the road toward the noise with their torches. I hope they are going to stop the truck. Others see me and rush in my direction. Their excited chatter sends me back into my car.

Buxom and wearing a going-to-get-married mini-dress, I feel naked and exposed. I roll up the windows and lock all the doors, except the one with the broken lock. I duck down, and hold my door closed.

Animated, the men surround my car and peer inside. In the dancing light of their torches, I look up and see their faces — decorated with scars and tattoos, their teeth filed into points. They are knocking on my window, pounding on the car, yelling as the sound of the oncoming truck intensifies. It's not going to stop.

Acting quickly, the men push the car out of the way. I slip it into neutral and they almost lift me off the road! Just in time! The big noisy tanker crashes past in a blur of sand

and diesel smoke. The driver sounds his horn in a fit of anger. That was too close!

As the air clears, I register that these men have saved my life. They knock again on my window and talk to me in a language I've never heard before — it isn't Swahili. I cower in my seat — feeling vulnerable, frozen with indecision. How should I handle this? Maybe if I just stay put they will go away, and I'll just sleep here for the night.

One of them opens the engine hood in the back, while others start looking through my stuff, which lies scattered on the ground. An older man, whom the others call Kanu, looks through the windshield and motions for me to try the ignition. I turn the key and a shocking barrage of sounds erupts, so I turn it off. Wanting to get inside, Kanu tries the passenger door, which is locked. I remain rigid as I try to assess what my choices might be. If I sit here until morning then what? They might go away. They might roll my car over. Or maybe set it on fire. I am thinking craziness here. Why would they do that, having risked their own lives to rescue mine?

Dizzy with fear, I open my door. Summer jobs acting in children's theatre kick into play. I emerge from the car, clown-like, bowing and throwing kisses of gratitude. From the perplexed looks on their faces, I ascertain that they have no idea what I'm trying to say.

So, I embellish my performance using mime, acting out my whole story, which I recount to myself in English. "Here I am, happily driving through the night, singing to myself, rolling down the window, nervous because I can't see. Then I hear strange sounds coming from my engine as it chokes and sputters and ultimately stops dead!"

I provide sound effects, which they like. They are visibly amused as I continue to animate each action. "I hop out of the car and try to push it but it is too heavy, so I throw everything out, madly, in a rush to avoid a horrific collision with — what do I hear? A lori kubwa — a big truck!"

They have grasped that I am a buffoon and love it. I am warming to my audience. "I kick my car, calling it "Dudu kufa! Dead bug! Bad dead bug!" as I do all the actions, pushing the dead weight. They cheer me on.

"Then suddenly I stop — big men with big muscles are coming toward me! Frightened like a mouse, I jump back in the car and hide. Taking a peek or two out the window."

They get it; they think I'm hilarious. Thank you, Mother of all Muses! Surely they won't kill the clown.

Remembering that I am in this ridiculous outfit, I grab one of my African cloths and wrap it around myself, as we begin a gestured conversation about what could be wrong with the car, which looks like a wreck. When I bought it on the black market in Nairobi, it was like new. After having been chased by rhinos and crossing thousands of miles of roadless wilderness, the retreads are worn smooth and the body is pocked with dents.

They are all over Dudu now, inside and out. One young man hops in and steers as the rest of them push it further off the road and into the forest. I can hear the ocean as I trip into the darkness, following them. Clutching my purse like a little old lady, I try to keep up. A flicker of firelight up ahead makes the trees dance. I smell maize being cooked and it stirs my appetite. I haven't eaten for a couple of days.

The village is closer than I thought. All at once, I come out of the darkness into a colourful place. I am surrounded by people, some of them smiling, some of them nervously hiding behind others, not easy with having a stranger intrude. Though the women are topless, I feel underdressed. They wear boldly printed turbans and, around their hips, cotton kangas of bright, large patterns — orange against turquoise, red against white, black against yellow. Their arms and legs are adorned with beads and shells. The men, too, wear kanga cloth around their waists, though shorter, and kufis (caps) on their heads, which I assume means that they are Muslim. Children stare at me from the shadows. A couple of daring women pull me toward the fire.

Some young boys sneak up from behind and try to grab me inappropriately, and I do my angry dog routine, growling at them. They jump back, startled, but are quick to muster up the nerve to heroically try again. I take the offensive and jump at them, growling and barking wildly. They are convinced that I will bite them. I suspect that they think I am mad. So, I play with them; let them get closer and closer, until finally I let them touch me on the head. That seems to go over very well. They giggle and clap when I start to pant like a happy mutt.

An older woman cautiously brings me water to drink. Could I be any more peculiar to them? I can hardly believe myself, acting so strangely, but I am desperate to keep this gathering congenial.

They seem delighted with my odd behaviour and wait for my next surprise. I look around and see mothers, some of them still teenagers, with babies swaddled in kangas wrapped against their bodies. Old men and women eat slowly, eyes locked on me, inquisitive.

It's a sizeable settlement with huts stretching into the darkness. Most of them are rectangular with low-hung thatched roofs. The paths reveal a tight web of community lacing the homes together. The big fire acts as the hub; all paths lead here. I am offered a cob of maize blackened by the fire, and I eat it with pleasure. They nod, approving of my appetite.

My car is being disassembled. I will not be going anywhere tonight. I fight my paranoia — I could disappear, and no one would ever know.

A crowd of men stands watching, as my car and all of my possessions are assessed. I am in no position to stop what is happening; I am at their mercy. For the time being, I don't want to leave the light of the fire for the pitch-black unknown.

I decide that my best option is to keep them amused. Clearing my throat, I am moved to sing an old camp song, which seems fitting, here by the fire:

Land of the silver birch, Home of the beaver,
Where still the mighty moose wanders at will.
Blue lake and rocky shore, I will return once more,
Boom-buddy-um-boom, boom-buddy-um boom, boom-buddy-um,
Booooooom.

They all nod and I repeat the "Boom-buddy-um-boom" phrase over several times. Magically, the women fall into singing it with me. I motion for them to keep it going as I add another verse on top. It sounds pretty good!

They are so easy with the music, immediately filling it in and making it bigger and more vibrant. It blossoms beautifully with their layers of sound, and they motion for me to stand up and sing out. A big woman stands up beside me and adds a harmony. Others ad lib. Children join in. Sticks become instruments of percussion.

"Boom-buddy-um-boom" has never sounded so rapturous and resounding. It's deliciously organic, so fluid, folding over and over itself with parts intertwining. I am singing against an intricate jumble of multiple parts that instinctively build to a mighty cadence. Wow! This is more thrilling than any choral performance I've ever heard.

Immediately, this gives way to another song that Kanu initiates by singing a phrase, which the others repeat with fearless embellishment. I join in. It is so spontaneous. No sheet music. No confining rules. No boundaries. No judgment. So unexpected. We are making music, rich in range and tone — I am thrilled when my voice melds with all the others.

Ever since I was a kid, I've loved to play around with harmonies and descants. People would make a fuss over me, believing I had a rare gift, but here it is anything but rare — it is as natural as breathing. Everyone improvises freely — even the toddlers.

Caught up in the moment, in the strength and passion of Kanu's voice, I belt out a response, mimicking their lyrics. The song dies in an explosion of laughter. What did I just say? Something hilarious? Crude perhaps? I can only imagine, but I can't help but join their fit of the giggles.

I glance over at my car. It seems that, amongst other things, they've decided to change my fan belt. Looking for a substitute, they have pulled a pair of nylons out of my backpack. I haven't worn them since I packed them back in Canada almost a year ago. I'm glad I didn't throw them out. I was going to wear them at my wedding. In fact, I had a whole outfit planned. Michael had bought a safari suit and a new pair of boots.

I see a brash young man playing with my camera and I can't help but feel anxious. Long and lean, he's wearing shorts made from cut-off dress pants, and the tattered remains of what was once a white dress shirt. The camera is full of exposed film, so I don't want him to open it.

My singalong pals follow my focus. Kanu tells the wannabe photographer, Hasani, to give the camera back to me. At least that is what I assume he is saying. Hasani rudely barks back at him, refusing, and a hush falls over the whole tribe. The two men argue back and forth, both of them digging in their heels. The singing stops and Kanu marches toward the young man, waving his stick. Hasani, who looks as if he is in his early twenties, bristles with defiance.

It is best that I stay out of this, I decide. The situation is finely balanced between young and old, and could tip either way. Kanu, I am guessing, was once a leader, but now is bent with age; his skin is loose and thin. How old he is, I cannot tell, but I can see that the people still respect him. Hasani, on the other hand, is the most outspoken amongst the young and does not bow to Kanu's command. I can tell that individuals are choosing sides. This is not just about the camera, I am guessing. It's about what to do with me. And my stuff.

Hasani pushes past Kanu and walks toward me, a sneer on his face. I will myself to appear fearless. Is he going to hit me or give me back the camera? He stops at arm's length from me and we stare at each other, eyeball to eyeball. I feel that he is challenging me, but have no idea what I'm supposed to do. So I do nothing; I refuse to blink or lower my eyes. Maybe I am asking for trouble.

"What are you doing here?" he asks, in perfect English.

Stunned, I stammer the obvious, "You speak English?"

"No, it's Latin," he says scornfully. "You didn't answer my question."

"I'm on my way to my brother's — he lives in Tanga."

He doesn't quite believe me. "What's your brother doing in Tanga?"

Being aware of the expatriates and "do-gooders" from all around the world who live a privileged life here, I am careful about how I answer his question. "He's teaching Tanzanians to be schoolteachers."

"Ah. Teaching what? British history? Getting big money, no doubt."

"My brother teaches science. His family is with him — his wife and two children. They have been in Tanga for three years. They speak Swahili." I'm trying desperately to win his trust.

"Science. Good for him." He doesn't reveal how he feels about what I have said. Everyone yammers at him to translate, but he ignores them. Instead, he boldly states, "I think you should give us this camera. You are rich. You can buy another camera. If you want us to fix your car, you will give us the camera." He plays with the latches and the lens.

Actually, I think that's fair but it's not so simple. "Please don't open it. It has pictures inside that are important to me."

"More important than your car?"

"No, but the camera was a gift and ... I want to take more pictures ... of my brother and his family."

"Doesn't your brother have a camera?" Hasani grins, knowing he has a point and my arguments are feeble.

"It is my camera. I'm not rich," I say weakly. "I have a clock you can have ... a radio or anything else."

He grimaces at my limp attempts at compromise. He opens my camera and takes out my film, ruining it all by exposing it to the light. Maybe he doesn't know much about cameras and film. I try to remember what pictures were on this roll. Most of them were of Michael and me — the dig, working back at the museum, sorting out the bags of artifacts, decorating our apartment, shopping in the markets. The good times. Gone now. Wiped out for good. That's metaphoric.

The people are getting agitated now, not understanding what is being said. Kanu tries to take the camera, but Hasani slaps his hand away. That brings more men into the fray; the mood is getting tense.

Cheerily, I try to speak to everyone through Hasani. "Would you thank them for me please. Everyone. They have been very kind, to feed me. Rescue me." Some of this I say in Swahili with the hope of being understood. Some of them do, and some of them nod. Hasani eyes me with suspicion.

"You are American?"

"No, Canadian."

"I hate Canadians."

I am surprised. His friends are now playing with my radio, my cassette player, and are rummaging through my toiletries and underwear. A bathing suit flies through the air, and Hasani catches it by the crotch. It's very pink. He plays with it like a puppet, and mimics my voice, "Hello, I'm a Canadian. My brother does good things for the poor people!" He repeats it, I'm assuming, in their language. I can feel his power within the group build as they enjoy his mockery. He has a gift for entertaining and the crowd is now his. Kanu, the old man, stays quiet and looks to me to do the same.

I feel the cold sweat of fear. Hasani dumps my undeveloped film out of the bag. I want to grab it back, to save it. Children can feel the tension brewing and crawl nervously into their parents' laps, as if suddenly I'm to be feared or detested. I have lost my audience.

A young man masterfully slams away on one of my drums, making it resonate far beyond what I could do. It sounds big and beautiful, even melodic. I bought it in West Uganda in a small town the very day Idi Amin pulled off his military coup. The people in that town were celebrating, and I being naïve at the time, I danced and played with them. Over the following week, I witnessed chaos in the streets of Kampala while taking refuge at the Girl Guide Centre. Happily, I was able to get out of the country, but not before being searched and harassed a number of times. That experience has made me cautious; I know things could go badly here.

Some of the younger women quietly leave with their babies; perhaps they have been dismissed. I feel the adrenalin rushing through my body. What can I do to keep this situation from getting ugly?

"You have a beautiful village," I say to Hasani in a loud voice. A baby cries from one of the nearby huts and I stand up, trying to be casual. "My mother was born in a handmade house made of grass and earth. Not so different from your houses here."

I walk over and touch the closest mud hut. "My grandfather built a house like this one in the wilderness, in Canada, where there were no trees for miles, no people — just wilderness. He knew it would get very cold in the winter, so he made the walls thick."

They are all curious, wanting to know what I am talking about. Hasani reluctantly translates as I continue. "Where I come from, the snow can be this deep." I illustrate, using all the body language I can. "I come from the far North, close to the North Pole, where we have snow on the ground for eight months of the year. Sometimes we have to dig ourselves out

37

through the roofs of our houses because we cannot open the door."

There is a collective "Ah!" of wonder. I am winning them back.

"The next house my grandfather built was from trees he cut down and dragged to his land with his horses. He stacked them like this." I use maize cobs to demonstrate the construction of a log house. Then he put mud and grass in between the cracks." My audience moves in a little closer to see what I'm doing.

"Didn't he have servants?" Kanu asks.

"No, no servants. He was with his three brothers. They did everything themselves, and in the first winter, it was so cold that their cows froze solid, like ice statues, right where they were standing. Eyes still open." I mime the frozen cow statue with eyes bugged open. I might be exaggerating a little, but they like it. "The laundry that they hung out to dry, turned hard, like wood. The water, you see, turned to ice, just like that." I snap my fingers. "Everything freezes in the winter — we skate on the rivers and lakes. We can even drive on them with trucks and make holes in the middle of the lakes so that we can fish. Sometime the ice is this thick (I stretch my arms out) and we can see the fish swimming beneath us, through the ice!"

Even Hasani seems mildly interested in this, but the guys over at my car have found something. They call out to Hasani, telling him what they have discovered and he looks at me, puzzled. "You have a bullet hole in your hood."

"I do!?!" Shocked, I try to think back to when it might have happened. "Well, I was in Kampala in January and there were a lot of guns going off. And my car was parked outside for days ... the tires all went flat. Soldiers —"

He cuts me off. "Are there any guns in the car?"

"No! Of course not!"

Hasani gives them some quick explanation and then urges me back into the story as the mechanics go back to work pulling out the fuse box.

He asks, "Why was your grandfather living in the wilderness?"

I explain how my grandfather, a city boy with eleven brothers, left his home in Colchester, England, at the age of seventeen to travel across the ocean to the New World. His parents couldn't provide for him, so he had to find his own life, a better life. He had to learn how to farm and hunt in order to survive. My mother grew up eating deer and moose and wild birds.

Hasani translates to the others. They can relate to this hunter lifestyle and nod with respect. Curious, they ask more questions, and come closer to me.

"While travelling west across the great plains of North America, my grandfather met my grandmother and they fell in love. They were married for over fifty years and had six children."

Hasani sits down near me. "And where were the black people?" he asks dubiously.

"Well, I never saw a black person until I was about nearly finished school. I went to a baseball game, and there was a team from a town up north that was mostly black. I remember that they won the tournament. But there were none in my school. We had students whose parents were from Japan, China, India, Greece, Italy — from all over the world, but not Africa."

"What were these black people doing in Canada — what kind of work?"

39

"They came to farm — just like my grandfather. They came up from the United States."

"As free men?"

"Yes, of course."

"Did you ever have slaves in Canada?"

"I don't think so. But I know that slaves used to escape to Canada ... long ago."

I wish I could think of more to tell him. My knowledge of Canadian history is minimal — I know more about Britain and the United States!

"And these baseball players played against the white boys?" Kanu interjects.

"Yes, they did."

"What about the Indians? You had Indians. Where were they?" Hasani presses me again.

"Well, where my folks grew up, there weren't many Indians. At least I didn't hear much about them. That's a good question! Where were they? When I was growing up, in the city, we had some at my school, but just a few. Maybe there were more, but I couldn't tell. Nobody ever actually said to me, 'I am an Indian.'"

I could have asked, I realize. Like everyone else during the 1950s, I was in my own little world, taking everything for granted. Mom was a full-time homemaker, Dad, a good provider. Life was easy for me until my father died suddenly, and my world fell apart.

I decide to change the subject. "Growing up, I had a horse — what we call a mustang, an Appaloosa, white with brown spots. I kept her at my aunt's farm north of the city, where I lived. There was a school for Indian kids just a few miles away from the farm and I used to ride over there sometimes. The children

40

came from places where there were no schools. They lived in a huge brick building together — out in the middle of nowhere."

"Without their parents?"

"Yes. It was not a happy place. There was a graveyard with plain white crosses planted in a row. There were no names on those crosses, just numbers."

"Was it Catholic?" Hasani asks — as if he already knows.

"I think so."

"There were places like that in Africa. Boarding schools." He can relate.

What an odd place that school was, when I think of it. I change the subject.

"In the summer, I did some barrel racing. You know what that is?"

"Racing barrels?"

I laugh. He has a sense of humour. "No, racing around them. On a horse." I draw a diagram in the sand, and describe how the ponies turn so sharply, at such an angle that they sometimes fall over.

"So, Indians and Whites live separately in Canada?" he persists.

"Mostly, but Indians are free to come and go as they please, I think. Like I said, we had some in our school, but most Indians lived on reserves — big pieces of land. I've never been on one. But, no, they didn't work like servants, like here ... it was different. Not fair, but different."

"Did they farm?"

"I don't think Indians ever farmed. The ones who lived near my city were Cree — that was their tribe. They were hunters. Trappers. They lived off the land."

That's all I know. Even that, I'm not sure of, but he keeps

asking questions. "Yes, they can be doctors or teachers if they study, though I don't know of any."

"Did you grow up with servants?" he pushes to know.

"No. We cleaned our own houses. We planted our own crops. And ate from our own gardens. My father and brothers go hunting in early autumn. We fish in the lakes."

"That sounds pretty good, I guess." He softens a little. When he smiles, he's handsome. We hold our look and stay with the quiet for a moment, until it's uncomfortable.

Then I ask him, "What about you? What's your story?"

"I went to school in Dar es Salaam. I lived with my auntie, my mother's sister. I had a teacher from Canada there, who said I was smart. He said I could be anything I wanted to be. But it was hard. My auntie lived outside the city, so I had to walk five miles to school and back, every day."

"That was tough, my goodness!"

"I thought I was lucky. My teacher said he would take me to Canada one day. I believed him. I did favours for him." He doesn't translate to the others, but they all sit quietly out of respect. "I found out," he continues, "that he was promising several students the same thing, and they were doing favours for him like me. Too many favours."

"What kind of favours?"

He looks at me as though I am dim-witted and I realize what kind of "favours." "Oh. He was a real bastard. I see." I say this with a pleasant expression, so the others won't guess. He smiles ever so slightly at me. He's not going to translate this conversation. It's between him and me now.

"Yes, he was. So, I quit school, and I came home. This is where I belong. This is where I like to live, where I trust the people. Now you tell us another story."

"I will tell you all a story, and you — I gesture to all of them — tell me your stories. They don't need to be long stories —"

"We have excellent stories." He cuts me off, a little defensive. "We have many stories, short and long. We will tell you story for story."

"Good. Good, that seems fair."

So, we begin a volley. All through the night, we trade stories. And what amazes me is that, from this firepit on the shores of the Indian Ocean, my country seems more extraordinary to me than ever before. Growing up, I thought it so ordinary. I dreamed of living in Europe and other exotic places. Like Africa! What I tell them now about my country seems as exciting and strange to me as it does to them. I come from a place where grizzly bears come down from the mountains in the spring in search of food after sleeping for months; where ice fog hangs in the air so thickly you can't see your own feet; where sap that weeps from the trunk of a maple tree is boiled into syrup, then thrown into the snow where it turns into candy.

I tell stories about my youth, my family, the people I know. I used to stand up bareback on my horse and race my cousin across the endless, empty flatlands where hundreds of thousands of buffalo used to graze. Now the buffalo are all gone. I realize that as a kid I had such freedom; we could stop and camp wherever we wished and nobody worried. As long as we did our chores and got good marks at school, we were pretty much on our own.

I tell them about my godfather who wandered the far North, where the sun never sets in the summer and never comes up in the winter. He was looking for gold. For decades he lived with the Eskimos — as they were called in those days — who taught him how to survive. He learned how to build a house from a particular kind of snow. I explain that to people in the North, there are many kinds of snow, such as snow falling, snow on the ground, and snow used to make houses.

We have indoor swimming pools that are heated by boilers all through the long dark winters, and stock car races where drivers smash into each other on purpose. Our cowboys and cowgirls drive the cattle up into the highlands in the summer and bring them back to the ranches for the winter. Our soldiers have fought wars on the other side of the planet against people they knew nothing about — some of them never came home and nobody knows what happened to them.

In return, they tell me about clearing huge tracts of land for the sisal plantations. Kanu's grandfather worked for a German who brought the first plants over from Mexico in the belly of a stuffed crocodile. Some of them spent their lives building churches for missionaries who told them that if they believed in Jesus, they would never die. In the early days, many members of their tribe sailed off on trading ships and didn't come back. Nobody knew what happened to them. They tell me about racing ostriches and about dolphins that come to the sound of drumming, chasing the fish into the small bays so people can catch them with their bare hands. They tell me about squid who remember wrongdoings and seek revenge, about boats washing up on their beaches — some of them ransacked by pirates. Others mysteriously empty of people but full of food.

After several hours, I am offered a drink of tombo, a strong home brew, and the questions become more personal and direct.

"Yes, I was expected to get married at around twenty-one years of age and I was expected to be a virgin." That is so funny and extraordinary to them that I have to say it a number of times in a number of ways before they comprehend.

"How could a woman be a virgin when she is so old? Are you a virgin?" they ask seriously.

I am red-faced and try to laugh it off. "That is too personal." Hasani can't translate *personal*. But he says something that satisfies them for now.

"Do you go to church?" someone asks. I admit that I rarely do.

Some women tell me that they start having sex when it's natural — when it is meant to be. That is the way they are made. When you are hungry, you eat. When you are afraid, you run. When you want to mate, you mate. The Christians told them that they had to wait for permission from God or they would go to Hell — but then, those who didn't wait, didn't go to hell or anywhere, so they began to question the power of this "God." One woman my age has six children. Most have three or four. Hanu and his wife, Leela, have many great-great-grandchildren.

"Yes, I am twenty-four and not married. No, I don't have children. Yes, that was my choice. Of course, I use birth control."

What a sorry specimen I must be in their eyes. A woman of twenty-four with no children, who takes pills to prevent a pregnancy. They have never heard of birth control. They want to have children — it's a measure of their worth, it's a source of happiness, and it's part of life's journey. It's the whole point of being alive, Leela tells me.

I don't make sense to them. "What are you doing here, all by yourself? Where is your family? Where are you going? Why did you leave? What are you looking for here?" The simple questions are the hardest to answer. Why did I leave my widowed mother at home to live alone? I stammer and contrive answers that are impossible to defend. I realize my mother must be wondering what has happened to me. By now she must think I am married. I will have to send her a telegram telling that I changed my mind.

Suddenly, I miss her terribly.

Here I see three and four generations sitting together, living together in tiny houses, while my family is scattered around the world. My mother sold our family home because her children moved away and rarely come home; there was no reason to have a big house. I have cousins I have not seen for fifteen years. I have degrees I may never use. Here they are struggling to build a school so that they can find work in a world that is quickly descending upon them. They know they must adapt, but what will be sacrificed in doing so?

In the early morning sun, I succumb to my fatigue and fall asleep by the fire. I wake up to hear my car purring like a happy cat. It is fixed and ready to go. Hasani shows me what they have done. They have made several new fuses and have repaired the circuitry with tin foil from cigarette packages. It should last until I get to my brother's home in Tanga.

Apparently, in Uganda, when I took my car into a garage to have my tires replaced and my horn fixed, the mechanic replaced the fuse with a bullet! Last night, when I heard the truck coming and banged on the honker, the bullet fired! Luckily, it was facing away from me.

All my stuff has been neatly packed inside my car and they have tied a huge basket of mangoes to the roof. I guess they noticed how many I ate this morning!

After many hugs, I offer them my camera, but they laugh

and ask me to take their picture. Unfortunately, I have no film left; it's all been exposed. Hasani apologizes with a shrug. "We will have to remember each other by the stories we have told," he says.

I look at their loving faces. The tattoos and filed teeth are secondary to how I see them now. "I will remember you all. Always. You saved my life."

"I am sorry if we scared you at first. You were strange to us."

"And you to me! I'm glad my car broke down! It was like a gift from the gods — exactly what I needed." I learned more about Africa in one short night than I had in the previous seven months. And I learned a lot about myself as well.

Hasani shakes my hand. "We will always remember the mwandishiwahabari from the far North, with her tiny skirt and her big voice."

"The mwandishiwahabari?"

"The storyteller. Yes, that is what you are!"

"Well, I never thought of myself that way before — but I like the idea. I loved what we shared last night — it lifted my spirits."

"That is how we will remember you," says Hasani, "and your extraordinary country. So different. I could not live like you, wandering about. I would feel lost."

"Sometimes being lost opens up new possibilities. It brought me to you." Hasani likes this idea; he thinks it is amusing. "But," I add, "I could not live like you either. I would be restless."

"If you were not travelling, and I was not here, we would not have met. We are both fortunate that our lives have crossed."

"Yes, we are."

I shake hands with every one of the villagers. The young boys try to attack me from behind, but this time I grab them and give them a "grizzly bear hug."

The old man, Kanu, seems sad to see me go. "Thanks for backing me up last night. I know it was difficult for you," I say to him. He holds my hand tightly and nods; he doesn't need a translation.

His wife gives me some beads. "She made from an aluminum cooking pot," he tells me. "She got it from some third-world aid program. But when she cooked with it over an open fire, everything burned."

"Asante. I will keep them forever."

My world has shifted. I feel like I am leaving one life behind and starting another. This visit has been a transition of sorts. And being with these people has made me hungry for the prairies, for my family and friends. With a sweet sense of optimism, I am going home. Everything seems possible again.

As Dudu and I head down the road, I hit my horn and it works! I see the villagers in my rear-view mirror, cheering me into the future.

SYNCHRONIZING 16-MM FILM FOOTAGE TO SOUND, FILMWEST, 1977.
ANNE WHEELER ARCHIVES.

DOWNSIDE UP

Edmonton, 1972

IT'S AN ARDUOUS JOB synchronizing 16-mm film footage to sound, cranking the 1000-foot reels back and forth, finding the clapboard slates (when they exist) and lip-reading, trying to guess what people are saying, then finding it on the magnetic tape (when they don't). For hours, I've been down in the unfinished basement of our offices, standing at our makeshift bench, splicing and taping the takes together, when I hear the phone ringing in the reception area upstairs. Our office manager, Joanie, is not answering — she must have gone out, I guess. So, I leave the reels spinning and race to answer it, thinking it might be the guys calling from a pay phone down near Drumheller, where they are shooting today.

Maybe they need something.

Maybe it's my mom reconfirming supper.

Maybe it's a bill collector. Heaven knows we've been hearing from them a lot lately.

"Good afternoon. Filmwest Associates," I answer, in a cheerful, sweet voice, sounding like a receptionist in an upscale trendy office, rather than the tired and sweaty gal that I am.

"Hi ... is Dale in?" The voice is big and deep.

"Ah, no he isn't. Can I help you?"

"You the secretary?"

"Ah, no. She's not here today. I'm a partner here." I say this with confidence, though I'm not sure that the term *partner* is a legal one. We're a company, a collective, a co-op — depending on who it is we're talking to these days.

"A partner?" He pauses in disbelief. I hold the silence. "Well," he continues, "I'm phoning from the Saddle Lake Reserve, eh? Dale and I were talking about your company doing some filming up here. You know about this?"

I remember this guy. I think he's the chief. We had several meetings with him and different members of his council last winter — they have one of the most progressive reserves in Alberta and have secured some substantial grants, big money, to spend on educational initiatives. I had better handle this call very carefully — it could lead to something big.

"Of course I know about this," I answer, not mentioning that I was at those meetings. "You are developing your own curriculum and want to make a number of films in your own language. Fantastic project. We're very excited about working with you on this."

"Oh ya?" He sounds encouraged. "Well, what we want is for one of your guys to come up here and do a bit of filming. Tomorrow."

"Tomorrow?" I stutter. "What's happening tomorrow?"

"Well, tomorrow is the beginning of something big. We're going to turn over the land, plough it up for the first time, eh?"

"Really! First time? That is historic." I mean it.

"Ya. Our people ... we were never farmers but things change, eh? We are trying to find a new way to live off this land. Going into the farming business, planting crops. I talked to Dale about this and he said I should call and let him know so we could try this filming thing out ... have a test run and see how we get along, you know?"

"Oh sure, of course. Good idea."

He talks on and on about the tractor they bought while I keep pondering exactly what I should say here.

"We thought we'd be doin' this a month ago, but there's been a lot of rain up here, so we had to wait 'til it dried up a bit. So send your cameraman here tomorrow morning. Saddle Lake Reserve. Okay?"

"Sounds great." I muster some assurance. "We'll get someone up there with a camera. What time?"

He doesn't respond. I wait for a moment and can hear him talking to someone else, but can't make out what he's saying — he must have his hand over the receiver. Then he comes back on the line. "Where's Dale?"

"We're doing a film for the National Film Board of Canada south of Drumheller, about three or four hours from here. He's with the crew."

He doesn't respond immediately. "Anybody else there?"

"No, just me right now. But don't worry. I'll call Dale and the other guys. We'll get this organized."

"You got a number for them?"

"No, they're on the road. They'll call in, but I can get this organized for you."

He's not easy with this. "When's he coming back? We're going to start early, eh? About nine."

I hear more muffled voices asking him questions. I can

hear him respond, "It's only her there; she'll speak to the guys later — they're on the road. We got no choice."

I'm feeling put down, so I decide to go for it. "Dale calls in every night," I lie. "We'll make it happen, don't you worry. We're all equals here," another lie, "and we make decisions together. If Dale said we'll do this for you ... as a trial shoot ... then we will."

He's still not happy. "Tell Dale to call me. I gave him my card," he says with finality.

"It might be pretty late."

He's already hung up.

I have no idea how I am going to pull this off. The guys, all eight of them, have taken every piece of equipment we own with them and are not due back for several days.

I leave a message for Dale at the hotel where the crew is staying, but don't expect to hear from him tonight. I can't wait — I know there are no 16-mm cameras available in Edmonton, so I'll have to hustle and get one flown in from Vancouver. It's an hour earlier out there. If I call now, they'll get a camera package on a plane first thing in the morning, and I can pick it up before heading north. I'm not sure how we will pay for it, but I can't dwell on that detail right now.

Dale does call back, curious. His first thought is that I have found something technically wrong with the footage they've been shooting. They sent it off from Calgary to Vancouver a week ago, and I'm the only one who has seen it. After reassuring him that the shots look good — but I wish they would remember to use the clapboard and not just roll — I tell him what I've done.

He's staggered. "No kidding! I've been waiting to hear from this guy for weeks. I thought they must have changed

their minds about us. He was talking about bringing someone in from the States." He gathers his thoughts and takes
charge.

"Listen, Wheeler, we need to impress these guys. If they
like what we do, it could set us up for years. We should send
Rico up to shoot it."

Rico is our best shooter. We all know that, but it's not the
way it's supposed to work around here. There are ground rules.
We all get paid the same, no matter what job we are doing,
and we rotate the jobs so that no one gets stuck doing something tedious (like synchronizing rushes) multiple times in a
row (like yours truly).

We present ourselves to the outside world as though we
are a political experiment, each receiving 250 dollars a month,
all work valued the same, but the reality is that some jobs are
more valued than others and some personalities have more
clout. So there is a hierarchy, whether we want to acknowledge
it or not. Being the only woman filmmaker, I am a little para-
noid and suspicious that I'm not in on every decision.

"You don't need to send Rico for this, Dale! I can do it."

For some reason, I have never been sent out alone with a
camera, though I have been everyone's assistant. Sometimes
I get to shoot second camera (extra shots for the film), and so
far my footage has turned out okay — not brilliant, but okay.
I just need more experience.

"Wheeler, we can't fool around here."

"I'm not fooling around here! If I were anyone else sitting
here in Edmonton, like one of you guys, there would be no
question. You're all working down there. And I'm here. Ready
to go. I've shot stuff. Nothing has ever gone wrong — except
for when I loaded the film in backwards — but that was more

than a year ago! You know and I know that it is long past my turn to shoot."

"Maybe, but that's not the point."

"Well, what is the point, then? We're a 'collective' remember?"

He stumbles for words. "Well, I've talked to this guy a lot and, ah, he has certain expectations."

"Expectations?" I am finding it hard to hold down my anger. "Like a bunch of guys going up there and doing something heroic together?"

"We've had a few beers. He's a good guy." That's the closest he's going to get to a confession.

I resist the impulse to verbally go for his throat. It will get me absolutely nowhere. Calming myself down, I try the reasonable approach.

"Look, Dale, you guys are in the middle of something, which is paying us, and it's important. Rico would have to get in a car right now and drive into the night to be up there tomorrow morn —"

"Rico says he could be up there tonight. Five hours." Dale interrupts.

I push on with my argument. "I doubt it. Then shoot all day? With hardly any sleep? Then what? Drive back down there? Listen to me. These guys just want someone to take a few shots of them tilling the soil. Riding the tractors. It's simple stuff. Shots of wheels going around, people cheering. I'll make it clear that this is a one-time situation and I won't be shooting their precious movies, if that should happen. I will underscore that you, Dale, are in charge here, though I thought we were all in charge here, but I guess I'm an exception."

"You're talking bullshit, Wheeler," he interjects in a

"brotherly" way, like I shouldn't even imagine that there is any disparity. Shame on me for exaggerating the situation and getting snarky. Well, I feel snarky and I'm not folding. I come back at him in a "sisterly" way. Sweet and unyielding.

"Listen, Dale, we wouldn't even be having this conversation if I hadn't answered the phone. He's the one who hasn't given us much time. But we can't stop the tractor now. We gotta move on this — I gave 'our' word. So, please — do what is right here."

"Wait a minute," he says uneasily. I can hear some of the guys coming into Dale's room as he explains the situation to them. They start to argue.

I press the receiver to my ear, trying to make out what is being said. I shout into the mouthpiece, "We are supposed to alternate, remember?" My ego has kicked in and I'm getting angry. No way are they going to take this away from me. "We take turns doing the jobs nobody wants to do, remember?!"

No one but Dale can hear me. I imagine him holding the phone away from his ear. Then everything goes quiet — he has put me on hold or something. I wait. He comes back on the line. "Okay," he says, sounding resigned, "we're together in this ... you are the shooter."

I think I'm going to cry. He continues in a more accommodating tone, "But what are you going to do about a camera, Wheeler? We can't send you one ... it won't get there in time, and besides we need both of them here. We have a big day tomorrow, with two crews shooting non-stop."

What were they arguing about then? That we should cancel and send nobody, rather than send me? Forget that. *"Stay calm,"* I tell myself. *"Not my hill to die on right now. I'm winning the battle."*

"I have a camera flying in from Vancouver tonight," I reply. "I'll pick it up on my way out of town. I had to phone them right away so it could get sent here in time."

He seems caught off guard and slightly pleased. "Oh! Good. What kind of camera?"

"A new Canon." I haven't a clue about this piece of equipment, but it was the only one they had. I exude confidence. "It's a snap to use, they said, "everything is automatic — light meter, focus, everything."

"Oh. Wow! Nice." Dale sounds positive. "How much are they charging?"

"Same as for their Eclaire. With a tripod."

"All you need is a Bolex ... it's too much."

"They didn't have a Bolex. They had this and only this. I expect it's on its way by now." I am stone-cold serious now; he'd better back me up.

"Oh. Well then," says Dale, "that's it, I guess. Good luck!"

"Thanks. Hey! Don't hang up." I need a little support here. "So, ah, maybe you could call this guy. He said he gave you his card. Tell him you are sending a real pro." I sound too sweet now, ingratiating. I hate myself.

"Sure. He doesn't know who's coming, right?"

"No. I just said someone would be there."

"Wish we could send someone with you. To help, that is. Do you want me to call around?"

"No. I don't."

"He didn't want sound?"

"He didn't mention it." Actually, I didn't think of it. Maybe I should have. "He implied that we had agreed to do this for free — you might want to talk to him about that. At least get something for the gas and the film and processing."

We're both trying to smooth things over now. "Do you need some cash?" He sounds concerned.

"No, I'm good." I am good, relieved, much calmer now. "I'll be fine. Trust me. It is supposed to be a glorious day. I'll get some great shots."

We hang up, and suddenly I'm shaky. I've been trying to prove myself to these guys who, truthfully, have been great. Really — I owe them. I knew nothing about making films before I started hanging out with them. With three older brothers, I guess I have a tendency to feel like a kid sister, and I have to pump myself up sometimes.

WHEN I CAME HOME from travelling in Africa, I was absolutely broke. My mom had sold the family home and had rented a suite in a low-rise. I was happy to stay in her guest room. I'd been away from Edmonton for almost three years and was keen to see if any of my old friends were in town.

The day after I landed, I called around and discovered that my friend, William, was back home, too, visiting his mom. I caught him halfway out the door, on his way to a wedding. Twenty minutes later, he picked me up and there I was, in the back of a jeep, drinking champagne with a group of guys I'd hung out with at university. We'd all gone our different directions and lost touch.

"How have you been, Wheeler? I thought you were teaching high school out in Vancouver?"

"Ya, I was. Did some theatre out there too … musical theatre. Hard to make it as an actor unless you go somewhere like New York. I liked teaching, but not marching band music. I got restless so I decided to travel some more — went to France, studied French, you know, stayed with a family … worked a little, then the plan was to circle the globe but I ran out of money halfway through Africa. And you guys?"

"We're making movies!"

"What?!? Far out!"

"Ya ... it's wild. Documentaries. About the West ... we've made a few."

"In fact, we need an on-camera interviewer for a little thing we're doing ... want to try it?"

"Of course! When?"

"Day after tomorrow."

"I'm in!"

It was that fast! I couldn't believe my luck. There was no pay, of course, but it would be so much fun, with guys I knew, great guys! And soon after that, they doubled up with another group of like-minded filmmakers, formed a new company, and called it Filmwest. I sort of slid in there, unnoticed.

It's been two years now since we set up shop in this old house, and for me it's been a self-guided degree in filmmaking. All of us have jobs on the side. I'm still trying to finish a master's degree, but I work as a teaching assistant at the university. We use most of our earnings from making films to buy equipment and to pay for the overhead, which includes an office manager. It's been a challenge, but we share what we know, read everything we can, and the rest we figure out by doing it. When you are paying for your mistakes, you don't make them twice.

I LOVE THE PROCESS of making films from beginning to end: identifying the issue, finding the story, writing the proposal, raising the money, doing the research, meeting the people, filming, editing, adding music, designing the sound. It is an unpredictable journey and the hours are crazy, but I am such an eclectic person that it suits me very well — except when I'm in the basement synchronizing rushes.

I have only shot film with the two movie cameras we own — a wind-up Bolex and a bigger Arriflex. Both of them are old school; everything is manual. You have to load them in a black bag, void of light, and figure out your f-stop and depth of field by using a meter and a chart. It is more of a science than an art sometimes; I've almost memorized the manuals. I figure that this automatic Canon camera should be a breeze with so little to do. "Just point and shoot," the guy said. "It takes care of everything. You don't even need a light meter!"

Our offices are in an old house near the U of A campus, and I live just down the alley in a sweet bungalow that I share with a couple of other students. It's a great old neighbourhood with big trees and mature gardens. On this beautiful breezy evening with crabapple blossoms raining down like feathers, I lock up and try not to worry about tomorrow. I'm going to my mom's for dinner, as I do every Wednesday night.

I drop in on my mechanic, Kostas, who strongly advises me not to drive my feeble Fiat out of the city. "The tires are treadless!" he warns me. "The metal is so rusted — it's like phyllo pastry. I could put my foot through the floor. This is a for-city-only car, Annie! It's Italian! Cheap. Listen to it." He opens the hood and it sounds like a threshing machine. "Everything is out of whack!"

"I know it needs a complete overhaul but I don't have the time or the money, so please ... do what you need to — check the tires for air, change the oil and all the liquids. You know what to do." I'm flirting. We both know it. "Just make it work better, Kostas. I'll drive slowly, carefully."

"What about your boyfriends, you have so many. Take one of their cars ... or get one of them to drive you."

"I don't have a boyfriend. Those are not my boyfriends — they are my business associates."

He gives me the once-over, like suddenly I'm worthy of consideration. I look like I'm ready for war in my army surplus pants, Frye boots, and hunting vest. "You're not bad-looking," he says, kindly. "You could have a boyfriend if you wanted —"

"My mother thanks you."

Since my dad died, my mom has asked very little of me. I'm just squeezing out a living, but I'm happy and am not looking for anything from her. Her financial situation is a mystery to me in any case. I think my older brother has been kind enough to give her advice and make sure her affairs are in good order.

I've never been able to figure out why she isn't playing piano in some kind of band. Sure, she was a doctor's wife but she plays honky-tonk piano like nobody else, lighting up the room with her laughter and her music. Her style is so raucous that you can't put a drink on the piano, 'cause she will rock it right off!

I have never seen her cry; that part of herself she holds in tight. I know she hates being alone, but she never complains. There is a whole lot I don't know about my mother, but we're close. She's why I came back to Alberta.

Unlike my cousins, I have not "settled down" with a man who would love and provide for me. The whole idea of marriage scares me. I don't know why. It's too complicated to figure out, so I don't. As soon as marriage becomes a possibility, I bolt.

Maybe I don't want to suffer the way my mother did when my father died, ten years ago. I have never stopped to consider how it scrambled my life as well. He was a strict but a much-loved and respected father; I was the only child left at home and suddenly there was no strong authority figure. Within a week of his death, I was back at high school, determined to graduate and not be dependent on my mother.

Growing up, she and I were a musical duo — I sang and she played. We were regulars at hospitals, veterans' residences, charity fashion shows, and the like, and I had assumed that in some way I would be a performer. I attended the Banff School of Fine Arts as a teenager one summer, and when I got home my dad and I had a talk. It was time to choose my high school courses for university entry. He insisted that I drop my drama and music options and pick up some extra sciences. So, without argument, I did just that. I never thought to question his authority.

A few weeks later, he had a massive heart attack and was gone.

Today, when I park behind Mom's walk-up, I hear her playing the piano with a joy that rings familiar. I remember being three years old, dressed up in frilly frocks like Shirley Temple with my pathetic, ultra-fine hair bouncing in sparse ringlets. I loved belting out the words to the old songs, trying to match her flamboyant style. Hearing her play like that again, I enter her apartment singing, "First you put your two knees, close up tight, then you twist them to the left then you twist them to the right." Louis Armstrong, move over 'cause we are off with gusto. "Walk around the room kinda nice and light, then you twist around and twist around with all your might." I do all the actions, dancing my butt off and she's delighted. "Spread your lovin' arms way out in space, then do the Eagle Rock with style and grace. Swing your foot around then swing it back. Now that's what I call 'Ballin' the Jack'!" I fling my hips to punctuate the ending and she lands a big ten-finger chord.

I don't notice that she has a visitor, until he claps enthusiastically, yelling, "Fantastic, absolutely fantastic!"

Aghast, I turn to face a short man with a newly barbered haircut, dressed formally in a suit, shouting "More! More!" Putting her hands on her knees, Mom abruptly gets up to introduce us. "Joe, this is Anne ... Anne, Joe." We shake hands. He's beaming, seemingly gobsmacked by his good fortune. Mom realizes she still has her apron on. She whips it off to reveal a smashing cocktail dress.

She's in a super mood. "Joe and I were out. We bought some wine. Both kinds."

My mind registers the word *we* with a shudder.

"Would you like some?" Joe offers.

"Sure!" I reply. "White would be good."

He has a bottle already open and the table is set. "So you're doing a master's degree, I hear?" I am aware of him looking at me and registering the work boots.

"Yes. Yes. Well I've finished the course work, and I'm doing the research, but I haven't finished my thesis."

"She's a teaching assistant," my mom calls out proudly. "She teaches teachers. Like her brother. And she has a radio show too, on CBC, for kids! Every Monday afternoon at two o'clock."

"Good for you!" He's trying too hard. "I'm at the university, too. I have a good job there — overseeing new construction." I nod, and he leans into me, conspiring. "I just love your mother. She is the finest woman I have ever met."

"How did you two meet?" I inquire.

"I live down the hall here, 352, suite 352. I saw her when she moved in and I thought to myself, now that is one classy woman."

I catch a glimpse of myself in the mirror, looking stunned and grubby. "I'd better wash up, Joe. I had to take my car in — had to buy a couple of retreads, and I'm filthy. I'll just be a minute."

I scoot through the kitchen past Mom. "Where's that dress I left here last time?"

She's relieved I asked. "Hanging up in the hall closet. All fixed."

"Thanks!" I grab it and rush into the bathroom. I can hear them talk, getting supper on the table, as I miraculously transform myself into a girl. It's not the first time I've "borrowed" her makeup and perfume, since I don't have any of my own. I realize I should have worn a bra. Oh well.

It's oddly formal as we sit down at the table, pulling out our napkins. "I'm driving up north tomorrow, near St. Paul, to do some filming." I have decided not to reveal that I'm going to an Indian reserve.

"Why?" my mother asks.

"We're hoping to get a contract — up there."

"Who is we?" asks Joe.

"We call ourselves Filmwest. We make films — about Western Canada mostly."

"It's like a hobby," adds my mother.

"It is not a hobby, Mom," I say evenly. "We have an office, and equipment. A couple of our shows were on television last year."

Joe turns to my Mom, "Have you seen any of them?"

"No," she truthfully responds. "I missed them. I don't know

how she can afford the time when she's so busy at school. But she manages, I guess."

"Well, it must be a lot of fun," Joe suggests. He wants me to like him. I appreciate his support.

My mother knows me too well. She senses my lack of enthusiasm in regards to my degree and makes eye contact, "Don't you quit school now."

"My thesis topic is being reviewed," I assure her. "I can't do anything until it's approved."

"You've been saying that for some time now," she adds. This is an old conversation between my mother and me. Joe is uncomfortable with our lack of consensus.

"Well, good for her for taking a job in the meantime. Too many young people are unmotivated these days ... travelling around, wasting time. How many people are in the company, Anne? Who's the boss?" he asks, pleasantly.

"Nobody is the boss really. There are ten of us. We're a collective."

"Ah. Like a — commune?" Joe asks. The word *commune* sticks in the back of his throat, like he's never said it before, as though it's blasphemy. The world is, after all, in the midst of a cold war and "communism" is the evil force. Maybe I should not have used *collective,* but I could not help myself. I knew it would test him.

"We're incorporated," I confirm our legitimacy. "We have offices on the corner of 88th Avenue and 110th Street."

He thinks for a moment, nodding. "Red brick house?"

"Yes! You know it?" He must have lived in Garneau. What a coincidence!

"We're tearing all those houses down next year." He speaks with authority. "The university is going to expand in that direction. The new law building will be going in on that block, big parking lot —"

"What?! All those beautiful old houses are coming down?" I'm horrified.

"Yes, well. They're beyond repair. Fact is they were not built very well in the first place. And not maintained."

I have to protest. "Those houses are historic sites. Nellie McClung lived on that block! So did the Mannings. I love that neighbourhood! I live on 87th!"

He is taken aback by my opposition. "Sorry," he says, with a quick glance to Mom.

"It's a terrible little place she lives in." She's siding with him, looking at me with that look that says, not here, not now, please.

"It's what I can afford right now," I say in my defence, "and it's close to the university, too close obviously."

"You'll get a good job as soon as you complete this master's." My mother softens. "Anne has always been a good student. Honours. Has a math degree."

The math degree has not been used much, except in situations like this. I see that he is impressed.

"Emily Murphy lived on the next block," I persist. "Do you know who she was?" I ask Joe.

"No. Maybe."

"She was a suffragette," says my mom, wanting to end the discussion.

"Right, and a judge," I add, "a *real* judge. The first woman judge in the British Commonwealth."

He shakes his head. "That doesn't matter. Those houses aren't worth saving."

Well, at least he's straightforward. He's honest, I'll give

him that, but I don't like it. I can see that he holds his opinion firmly and so I decide to withdraw. Mom's mood is wavering, and I want to see her happy.

I dish out the casserole. "This is great, Mom, I love this recipe — Heavenly Hash. Mom's a great cook, Joe."

"Oh, I'm sure she is! She raised four kids. Cooked a lot of meals, I bet."

Mom settles into her chair. "Yes," she says, "a lot of meals. I have four great kids. Proud of them all." She and I smile at each other. I can see that this man makes her feel special. I'll go with that.

I'M UP BEFORE DAWN and waiting at the airport long before the camera package arrives. The flight is late and the paperwork confusing, but by 7:30 I'm on the road.

Saddle Lake is 150 miles north, so I'll have to drive like spit to get there in time. I pull the manual and the camera out of the case; I'll have to figure out how to load 100-foot reels before I get there. The man said they snap right in.

The only film equipment I know is the stuff we have accumulated at Filmwest. Besides the cameras, we have some good prime lenses, a couple of light meters, three tripods, and a Lowel lighting kit. The guys tell me we have something called a dildo, which they use when they really need it, but I have never seen it and don't want to admit that I don't know what it even looks like. I learn by watching and try not to ask too many stupid questions; things have a way of revealing themselves. All I know is that a dildo must be small and not essential or I would have needed it by now.

Once I get onto the highway, I plant the manual on the steering wheel and find the diagram that makes loading the film look so simple. Trouble is, I can't get the camera open, which is step one. Traffic is sparse, which is a good thing. I swerve from one side of the road to the other, attempting to pry the camera open with both hands while driving with my knees. After a near-death experience, I pull over and park on the shoulder.

"For heaven's sake," I mutter to myself, "you have to know how to open the damn thing!" Frustrated, I examine the contraption and find the magic latch, which, at a standstill, is humiliatingly obvious. But loading the toy is tricky. You have to use a built-in blade to trim the end of the film, then thread it perfectly straight through the impossible-to-see opening. I do this several times, imagining the chief with the big voice watching me as I try to look like a "real pro."

Now I'm really late. The school buses are on the road, tractors are moving out onto the fields, and commuter traffic is heading into the city. I pull a brush through my hair and push my foot to the floor.

There's a crowd hanging around the tribal band office by the time I arrive. I find a parking place amongst the herd of trucks and get my gear out and ready. Nobody takes any notice of me. They are all looking up at the bright blue sky, squinting to see a tiny dot circling above them.

Suddenly it drops down, dangerously low, looking for a place to land. The people whoop and cheer as the small airplane lines up its course in the distance. Squealing with delight, students pour out of the school across the road, pointing and cheering as it approaches.

There's been a lot of rain, so the fields are bright green and wild with new growth. Shallow pools of water stretch off into the distance, reflecting the cloudless blue sky. I won't be surprised if the big new tractor, waiting on the side of the road, gets stuck. I pull on my big boots.

At the last minute, the pilot decides to land on the road and heads right for the crowd of onlookers. People scatter, some into the ditch full of icy cold water, as the flying machine descends upon them. The wings tilt this way and that, getting pushed around by air currents, on what appears to be a very calm day. Maybe the pilot is inexperienced, I think to myself. The plane lands and bounces multiple times before coming to a sliding stop just short of the tractor. I can't imagine anyone being so cavalier in an airplane. The guy must be a madman.

A few of the band councillors, looking more like cowboys than Indians, strut toward the plane, as the pilot hops out with a proud grin on his face. They heartily greet each other in a self-congratulatory way, laughing and slapping each other playfully, as they walk over to the new, huge tractor. I grab my loaded camera, shove half a dozen spools of film into my multi-pocketed vest, and hoist the tripod onto my shoulder. Taking large flat-footed steps, I march toward them, ready to work. It's a man's world up here, so I enter their circle boldly.

"Excuse me?" I say with the lowest voice possible. They barely look down at me, expecting perhaps that I am looking for the bathroom. "I'm from Filmwest ... I spoke with some-one on the phone yesterday? About shooting this important historic occasion?"

They don't say anything. They are frozen in disbelief.

"I believe Dale called you last night?" I continue, putting down the tripod, which is unbelievably heavy. One guy nods slowly. I guess Dale didn't say I was a female. "Are you Wheeler?" As he asks this, his voice rises at the end of the sentence.

"Ya. Wheeler. That's me."

They look around, as if I've come out of nowhere. The big voice from the telephone asks, "You alone?" I nod. At 5'4" I'm a midget amongst them.

"Yes, and you are —?"

He smiles, a handsome man, and sticks out his hand. "Just call me Chief."

The tractor driver is mounting up, getting ready for the momentous deed of plowing the virgin field.

"Can you tell me what's going to happen so I can get my camera set up?"

The men realize that it's me, or there will be no filming. One guy manages to say, "Nice camera." I dive in with, "Yes, it's new ... a Canon, takes a great picture. So what are you thinking here? Tell me what you want."

The chief shrugs, what can he do? "Well, as I was telling Dale, we're thinking aerials. We got over sixty thousand acres here, all of it wild ... so we've cleared about eighty acres this year, and our friend Ron here is going to help us out."

Ron, the pilot, grins at me. "This should be fun" is written all over his face.

Being terrified of heights, and prone to airsickness, I already feel nauseous. I'm going up in a plane with this goon?

A couple of guys are already taking off the passenger door and figuring out a way to strap me in so I can look straight down and get a good picture, clear of the wheels in the foreground. One guy sits on the edge of the seat, then reaches out and grabs the strut before putting his foot on the wheel joint base. "Once you're in the air, this is the best way to get clear of the plane. We use this set-up for sky-diving...."

"Well I'm a foot shorter than you and ... I'm not keen on

jumping, especially without a parachute ... so do you have a harness or something?"

"Oh ya. Sure."

They have this figured out, too. I climb up and they place the seat belt through my rear belt loop, but it's too flimsy. So then they starting taking off their own belts and ingeniously buckling them together to make a harness of sorts, which loops through a couple of handholds and seat mounts that seem pretty secure. I can't believe I'm going ahead with this plan. Basically, I'm going to hang out the door.

With as much authority as I can muster, I give the pilot some instructions. "It's important that you keep a steady speed and a constant distance from the ground, so I can frame up." He nods and says, "Sure thing!" I detect a slight smirk forming in the corners of his mouth. Am I imagining this?

"I need to reload after about five minutes of shooting. Please don't dip and dive while I'm doing this ... just go smooth ... it's like threading a needle ... I will have to do it five times." All the men are strangely quiet as they anticipate my fate. They seem to be in the same state of disbelief as I am, but nobody is going to shut this idea down. I'm going up. No guts, no glory!

An older man, who has been watching from a distance, steps forward and asks with concern in his voice, "Can you fly that plane with someone hanging out like this, Ron?"

"Oh ya, no problem," says Ron, "Some of those big guys get out on the strut and can't let go ... I have to fly all over hell's half acre before they either fall — straight down — or get back in. This girl is small ... I'm ready to roll."

Oh great. I practice climbing in and out of the seat holding onto the wing strut and finding a stable place for my foot just above the wheel joint until I'm convinced that I'm strapped in safely. I will have to manage the camera with one hand. Thank goodness it's small. There's just one last thing. "Let's tie my camera onto this handle here, so I don't drop it ... just in case." They hustle to please me. This is good. "When we're up there, always bank to the right, it will be easier to get a good shot down." Ron nods, as do the others, all in unison like a bunch of kids watching a bouncing ball. Are they having me on? I'm not sure.

I need a moment to myself. I'm also not sure how long I'll be up there, so I hurry off to the bathroom before takeoff. It's an outhouse and there's a lineup, mostly women. One older woman, wearing a bright pink nylon scarf, speaks Cree to the others, and they graciously insist I go ahead. "You going up in that plane?" she asks.

"Yes, I guess so."

"You're a crazy woman." She laughs. "Don't expect us to catch you if you fall out! He's a terrible pilot." Now they all laugh.

"Really?" I croak. "He's had accidents?" Hearing my fear, she holds my arm.

"He's a good boy, but he likes to show off. You just stop him if you think you are in danger, and make him bring you down."

Right. Thanks for being so reassuring.

Once I'm strapped in and the camera is hung on a rubber cord, the pilot starts the motor up. "Don't you find that camera heavy?" he asks me.

"No," I reply, "it's a little awkward to hang onto — doesn't have a real handle. It's not the one I usually use. But it's not heavy."

From the moment we lift off, I feel dizzy with fear and nausea. Thankfully, I haven't eaten anything today, because nothing is gradual about this ride. The plane rises and falls with every change in topography down below — from lake to forest, field to highway; it shifts up and down with the different temperatures, the different pockets of air. The smell of fuel is thick, wafting all around us. My eyes keep watering from the fumes and the wind is whipping around my head.

I can hardly see the tractor and the crowds in the distance. I shimmy myself closer to the edge of the seat, ready to hang out. He gives me a nod and banks radically to the right. I almost spill out the door, sliding sideways, grabbing onto the wing strut, clutching the camera, and landing on my foot as planned. The harness holds.

The camera is like nothing I have held onto before — it's difficult to keep the frame steady. I can hardly bring myself to look down — the view from up there really makes me whirly. The first roll of film is shot mostly with my eyes closed. We circle out and around so I can reload. The second spool falls to the ground — watching it disappear gives me vertigo. I crawl back into the plane to reload. My heart is pounding like a bass drum gone bonkers as I manage to get the next spool trimmed and threaded and the camera back on my shoulder. More than once, I drop the camera. Thank goodness it's secured, but it bounces around and I have to stretch out to grab it.

I swear we are flying hazardously low, right over the tractor as it heads out into the field, but maybe I am not capable of judging. Looking through the lens is discombobulating. Everything seems closer and faster. I keep the lens wide so the focus holds. I just hope I don't vomit on the spectators.

It was a good idea to shoot it from up here; it gives the event a huge perspective. Hundreds of people are waving and cheering as the plough cuts into the wild green grass, leaving a fresh dark line behind. Flocks of gulls drop in to feed on the critters that have been carelessly exposed in the tractor's wake. Children run alongside, hopping on and off the huge machine, looking like flecks of confetti from my eye in the sky. When I stop to look beyond what is directly below me, I am moved by the beauty of the country. The parkland is spotted with sparkling lakes flecked with miniature boats; the railway strings the towns and grain elevators together, like an endless necklace from one horizon to another. Sections of farmland are like quilted squares sewn together, framed by straight roads, and pinned down with dance halls and churches. Funnels of dust follow trucks down gravel roads, and amoebic shadows from the clouds crawl constantly across the land. What an awesome sight! How lucky am I to see this! I am overwhelmed with a sense of belonging. I feel I can see where my grandparents settled, two hundred miles southeast of here, close to the little town of Edgerton. This is the upside of taking this risk ... the downside is that it could be the last movie I ever shoot.

Below me is the distinguished and undisturbed land of these Cree people. This is what it all looked like less than one hundred years ago, when there were no fences, no farms, no ranches, no roads. Now the people of Saddle Lake feel they must cut into this soil and take control of Nature if they are to survive in this new world.

I also can see that the tract of land that is the reserve is dotted with marshes and sloughs, making it too wet for growing grain. It is not prime farmland. It is not even good grazing land. Who has advised them to do this, I wonder?

If the camera's light readings are correct and the footage is as dramatic as it feels, I will be euphoric. We swoop and dive and buzz around in circles, until I'm limp with fatigue and my brain is completely scrambled. A couple of times I release a squawk, but mostly I am able to contain my fear. I feel so relieved to finally announce that I am out of film.

We land to a clapping ovation.

It takes a few minutes for the men to get me disentangled. I stagger, comically, to cover up how I feel, and retreat to my car where I can finally sit down and breathe. A little boy runs toward me with the roll of film I had dropped from the sky. Miraculously, it is still in its package, unexposed.

Determined to complete the job with no stone unturned, I load up the camera one last time and, with a whirl of enthusiastic children, march out to the field to take every conceivable shot of the tractor and its entourage. One teenage boy is pleased to carry my tripod and helps me set up in different places. He's interested in everything I am doing, and I encourage him to learn about making movies. I'm sure there will be a place for him on a crew if the bigger project should ever happen.

My task complete, I emphatically announce that I am truly out of film and am heading out. The older woman comes over to me with a plate of food, but I have no appetite. "What's your name?" I ask her.

"Ruthie!" she replies.

"I'm Anne."

"Wheeler," she corrects me with a giggle. "I know the guy who phoned you. We're related, and we had a bet when you were taking off, eh? I won a carton of cigarettes ... so thank you for not quittin'. I knew you would do the job." She offers me a cigarette, but it's the last thing I want right now.

Windows down, music up, I drive my little Fiat back to the

airport and put the camera package and film I shot on the last flight to Vancouver. If the shoot is a wipeout, I'll hear from the lab tomorrow. If it's exposed correctly, we'll get the footage sometime next week, but that doesn't mean it's in focus or brilliantly composed – it will just mean that there is a picture. If it's a soft blur, I will retreat, possibly quit in shame, and give up this dream of being a filmmaker.

THE NEXT DAY, I drag myself over to the university for a meeting with my thesis advisor, Dr. A. Smith. His office is in a beige and boring building. I have tried to be excited about this degree, but I have to admit I would quit if there weren't a paying job involved. Spending another couple of years of my life researching and writing up an academic document that a dozen people might read feels pointless to me.

Dr. Smith is delighted to see me, taking off his big earphones, and making a space amongst the piles of books and recordings he is assessing. I've never seen him play any instruments, but you can't fault him on his knowledge of music. I know he finds it difficult to categorize my ideas and me.

My thesis is to develop a curriculum for teaching music that does not involve notation. It relies on students using their ears rather than their eyes to learn music. Only after they can play what they hear or compose do they write anything down. The purpose of notation is to keep a record of what has been created, so it can be retrieved when needed.

I am inspired by my mother, who plays fantastically, but doesn't read music very well at all. She plays much more expressively and uniquely when she is playing by ear.

I believe it's possible for everyone to make music, not just replay what others have written. What if we were taught art the way we teach music, with everyone doing paint-by-number? Dr. Smith is far from impressed by my approach because he argues, "There is nothing to bring the musicians together." His experience is entirely based on playing and conducting bands, following notation. He admits to never having played by ear.

He massages his brow. "Your proposal did not satisfy me or the committee as being realistic. It has to be reworked. And I need to decide whether or not I should hold a place for you next year or not." He is referring to my job as a teaching assistant as well as my academic future. "I can only have two graduate students," he adds.

I press on with my theory. "You know, I've done a bit of travelling, and everywhere I went, I made music with the people, without notation. Usually I sang, but sometimes I played some kind of instrument. Often there would be ten, twenty, thirty people playing together."

"Yes, simple music, repetitious," he states impatiently.

"No, not always." I'm a little defensive. "There were different approaches. Sometimes pieces would start out simply with a melody or a rhythm, and the stronger players would embellish it and break off, not unlike what jazz musicians do — while others would play a continuum of some kind. Sometimes it was a call-and-answer situation, like in Africa. Other times, musicians took turns performing solos, showing off their brilliance. It often moved far beyond my Toronto Conservatory skills, and there were no pieces of paper holding them together. The music brought them together. Listening to each other, and responding, brought them together."

"How then, would you present this thesis if nothing is written down?"

"Well, I'd like to do it on film."

"Absolutely not. You wouldn't be taken seriously at all."

"Possibly not. But I wouldn't be the first —"

"No," he interrupts me. "It's not worth talking about, I'm afraid. I won't accept a thesis done on film."

He pulls on his jacket and turns off his lights, ready to leave. "I have to be clear with you, Anne. I want to see something in writing by the end of the month ... something that can be examined and assessed. Something that has some real academic precedent. Look at the Manhattan Project — that is a fresh approach — or Orff. And. You'll have to commit to a full-time effort. We'll meet next Monday — same time."

"Yes, sir," is all I can muster before zipping out the door. I'm not good at combating authority, especially from an older man. I want to do something that makes sense to me. I thought it could be in the world of music, but music in high schools is centred on band music. Students should be sent out into the world with skills they can use for the rest of their lives, like singing. I have done my time talking kids into playing instruments they will never own — like tubas and bassoons — playing repetitive bass lines to keep the marching together. Surely there is another approach to music that would serve them better.

WHEN THE GUYS RETURN from Drumheller, every question they ask about the shoot convinces me that I made multiple mistakes high in the sky. Aerials, apparently, should be shot in slow motion, to soften the movement. And the light settings are tricky when you are shooting up at the sky, then down onto the dark forest. I didn't touch any settings, believing the camera was an automatic godsend as I clung onto it and my life. I am convinced I have completely messed up my big opportunity.

On Monday morning, the lab in Vancouver finally gets in touch. Mark takes the call. They report that the exposure is good, the film is clean, and they will be shipping it out on Wednesday.

"What else did they say?" I ask him.

"Well, they said it looked like you had gone for quite a ride."

"You mean, they said it was shaky, unusable?"

"No, they said it looked like you had gone for quite a ride."

"Was it in focus?"

"Didn't ask. Oh, and your mom called. Sounded nice."

"That's it?"

"Ya."

Mom wants to make sure I'm coming for dinner on Wednesday night. It's odd that she needs to ask. She sounds nervous. I wonder what kind of mood I'll be in, given my vanishing film career, but I say yes. I'm curious to know more about Joe. He seems so brazen, so contrary to her British ways. I wonder if she wants to distance herself from him.

WEDNESDAY COMES, and the dreaded delivery from Vancouver finally arrives. The film gets slapped into the split reel and put onto the projector. All nine of us find a place to perch as the light begins to flicker on our white wall. Alan brings the image into focus as the Academy Leader counts down — nine, eight, seven, six — to my hopes and fears.

The first shot is a rush of movement, starting on the ground as the plane takes off, slashing through a rush of people and trees, then wildly swishes to something that stops us cold. What is that?

The big blue horizon hangs on the bottom of the screen like a huge body of water. The green fringe of the Earth lies above it.

"It's upside down," someone murmurs in disbelief.

We stop the machine and the dark room erupts into a tumble of questions. Rico flips on the lights.

"They must have sent it tail out. Or ... no ... that wouldn't do it ... the numbers would have been ..."

"They don't make mistakes ... it comes out of the bath onto the core."

"No ... it's right side up. The head leader was right side up." Now Reevan is looking at the film stock itself. "The emulsion is on the right side ... the problem is not at their end." He has worked in a lab; he knows all this stuff.

I am silent. Confounded.

Reevan pulls out another reel, and sure enough, it has the same configuration. Head leader is right side up — followed by an upside-down picture. We all come to the same shocking conclusion.

"You held the camera upside down, Wheeler. All day," says Dale.

"No, I didn't! I couldn't have!"

"You did. It's the only answer. The only way this image could be inverted."

I don't want to believe it. We've all made mistakes but this takes the cake.

Rico has a thought. "Was it that new Canon ... with the magazine on the bottom...?"

"Ah ... ya. It was a Canon. The magazine is on the bottom, not the top? I mean ... it was awkward but ..."

"I bet it was." They all laugh. I am mortified.

Both of our cameras, most cameras, have the magazine on top, like Mickey Mouse ears. That's what a camera looks like to me. They all look at me, waiting for the obvious.

"Okay. I guess I held it upside down."

I feel like a complete imbecile and weakly suggest, "Can't we just flip it? Turn it right side up, show it backwards or something?"

"You can't flip it, and backwards is backwards. The tractor will be going backwards, the plane ... never mind. No. That is not an option."

"Of course not."

Alan is sympathetic, "And it's single perf, right?"

"Ya."

"Too bad. It can only be threaded into the projector one way. If it was double perf, with sprocket holes on both sides, we could rig something up. The graphics would be backwards but —"

"But," Dale clears his throat, "these guys are coming down tomorrow to see this stuff. I already called them. They want to talk turkey."

It's a nightmare, worse than I could have imagined.

"Well, we might as well watch it upside down, and get some idea of what we have here," suggests Mark cheerfully.

"No," says Reevan. "Let's not get it all scratched up. We may need to make a dupe neg or something."

I have no idea what Reevan is suggesting, but it sounds expensive. And he is the most experienced filmmaker amongst us.

"We'll just tell them the truth — the girl held it upside down!"

"No, no, no!" I beg.

Mercifully, someone suggests, "Let's just have them come in and hang upside down from the pipes like bats in a cave ... that would work...." It's the best idea yet.

"Well," says Dale, "a reshoot is impossible of course ... even the land can't lose its virginity twice."

I put the film back into the cans, craving a solution. I have spent a lot of money and have cost them a potential contract. What can I say? "Sorry" is insufficient. I'll just leave with my tail between my legs.

For reasons I don't question, they keep spitballing. Ideas fly back and forth. "We could try mirrors maybe." "How would we do that? It's impossible — we don't have the room." "What if — what if we turn the projector upside down?"

The talk stops. We all think it out in our heads, then there is a "collective" Yes!!!! We could bolt the projector to the ceiling. Yes!!!!

We're on our feet now, figuring out how exactly that would work and where to set it up. We chatter back and forth.

"The reels won't work upside down."

"We'll have to manually crank them. It could be tricky."

"Then we have to change reels of course. How many are there?"

"Three," I say. "The third one is shorter."

"This could be a comedy routine!"

"If we hang it inside the closet, we can put curtains across this doorway and hide the projector and whoever is hand-cranking the take-up reel."

"Ya, we will just have the lens sticking out ... whatever happens behind the curtain, stays behind the curtain."

"The audience will be facing the other way."

"It will be noisy!"

"So, we'll find some very loud music!"

I am so relieved. They are not sending me away in disgrace. I am still included. This is a team sport and I'm one of the players. I am so moved, I can hardly speak. I'd expected them to give me a much harder time. I have learned something here — my assumptions have been unfair. I am at fault but no one is blaming me. There isn't any time to point fingers.

I help roll the projector to the other end of the basement and dismantle the editing bench so there is more space. The power drill is retrieved, along with some brackets and iron bars.

"What we need here is the dildo," Dale says in all seriousness. "Can you get that, Wheeler?"

"The dildo?" I ask weakly, not knowing what I should look for and why we would need it. I look pathetic. They all start to laugh.

"What? What is it? Show me what it is … I don't know. I give up."

I have learned about the equipment by watching and doing but this one piece has me baffled. "Really, is it something we can use here — to bolt the projector to the ceiling?"

They try to pull themselves together but refuse to let me in on the joke. I guess, in a fashion, they are getting back at me for this possible disaster.

"You're not going to tell me? Why not?"

They can't look me in the eye. "Ah … I think it's not here," says Mark, "It wasn't, ah, working very well, and I sent it off to be fixed. We really never used it much. We should get rid of it, don't you guys think?"

They all grunt accordingly. "Besides," Dale adds, with a straight face, "it could be dangerous if you used it upside down." That really cracks them up. What a bunch of brats. If I were more confident I would press them further, but clearly I will have to wait.

Rico, who is about to drill holes into the beam above him, turns to me and asks me directly, "Can you sew?"

"Not very well, but yes. I'll take care of the curtains."

I find an old pipe for a curtain rod and I take a few measurements before I leave.

SUPPER IS ON THE TABLE when I arrive at Mom's. I'm starving, so I dive right in. I don't notice at first that she is not eating and is strangely quiet. She says she's not hungry, so I help myself to seconds as she finishes a smoke. Butting it, she clears her throat, "Joe has asked me to marry him and I've said yes."

I swallow twice and then squeak, "Already?"

"It's been long enough. He's a good man, an honest man. And we enjoy each other's company. I've told your brothers and we're all going out for supper next weekend."

I put down my fork and get a drink of water from the tap. It will take a moment for me to absorb this shocking piece of news. She doesn't sound really excited, but I sense a calmness and contentment, which is good.

"He has a cottage up north," she tells me. "We've been fixing it up, and he loves to fish, you know. And I like it up there. I like his kind of life. I am more at home in the country. And he likes to dance. I like to dance. He's good for me —"

"Mom. You don't have to explain anything to me. If this is what you want to do, then I'm happy for you. Really. But do you have to get married?"

"Yes. Of course I do. I'm old-fashioned. I have to get married."

"All right then. When's the wedding?"

"You're not invited."

"Oh!"

"We're having a civil wedding with two witnesses, and then we're going out for a nice steak dinner."

It seems like she is leaving home, not me. It's backwards somehow. Why is she so anxious? Did she think I'd disapprove of her?

"If that's what you want, Mom, and you've decided, then I'm thrilled you have found someone you want to live with for the rest of your life." She takes that as a question.

"Yes, we'll take care of each other. He treats me with respect, and —"

I come over and give her a hug. "Good, good," I whimper, suddenly feeling very alone. For no good reason, I tear up and smile at her. She is uncomfortable with my emotion.

"I'm glad you understand," she says. "I hope you grow to like him."

"If he does well by you, Mom, that's all he needs to do. I'll like him a lot."

Nothing more needs to be said. I do understand and I will not challenge him again. I grab a Kleenex and blow my nose.

She takes my hand. "You know I will always love your father. He was the love of my life."

"I know that, Mom. You deserve to be loved. To be happy. I know you've been lonely. And I haven't always been there for you."

"You did your best." She sees I am tearing up again. "It was hard, losing your dad so young ... and I wasn't always at my best." We both start to cry. Embarrassed, she grabs a Kleenex too and we both blow our noses.

"So," I say, trying to change the mood, "I have to ask."

"What?" she says, ready for anything.

I could ask her what she thinks of me quitting school, but that can wait. "Do you still have that sewing machine? I have to sew something."

"Sew!? You?"

"Ya. I bought some material down at Zellers. Remember you sent me to that Singer sewing camp that summer after grade nine?"

"You hated it, I know."

I go to the front hallway and retrieve the bag of material. She is amused. "And I bought you a fancy machine. You used it as a hat stand. You told me to give it away ... to get rid of it."

"And did you?"

"No."

"Good."

"You are taking up sewing now?"

I lay out the cloth. "I have to make curtains."

"Curtains? You never cease to amaze me."

"Sorry. I know. I failed home economics. I never got the zippers straight. I hated buttonholes. One has to like something to be good at it ... don't you think? If you really want to excel at something?"

She knows where I am heading. "You are going to quit school, aren't you? I know you don't like it." She's no slouch, my mom.

"Well, I had a good idea, but my advisor is not keen and I'm not excited about doing something that well, you know ... I need to feel passionate about what I'm doing."

She nods. "It's a wonderful thing to do something that you love ..."

We're different but the same. She looks at me, really looks at me. "If you have the chance to make a living doing something you love, then do it now while you are still single. Life goes sideways, I can tell you that. And soon you won't have a choice — so do what you want to do while you can do it."

I feel that she's talking about herself here. "Was playing in that band, during the war ... something you loved?" I've never asked her that before. She seems stymied. It's hard for her to answer.

She nods, "It was. I mean ... your dad ... I didn't know if he'd ever come back, so I was in a constant state of worry ... but ... I loved the music. I did. And the musicians — they were so good, taught me so much. And I was learning new songs all the time — we got better and better."

"Is that what you would have done ... if you hadn't had me so soon after Dad came home from the war?"

She is unnerved by my presumption, but I can tell there is some truth in it.

"It was much more complicated than that," she says. "Your father was sick, and my life, like everyone else's life, had to shift — it was a new world. We had all lived through a depression, then a war. This was a chance to stop — and to settle down — but yes, I loved playing with the band. I did."

For her, that is a substantial confession. She wipes her hands on her apron and takes a breath. "I will go get the sewing machine."

THE DARK GREEN CURTAINS hang across the doorway — my sewing is not stellar but that goes unnoticed in the shadows. No one would guess that it is a contrived situation. There is space enough behind the curtains for two people to crank the reels so that the film will be taken up after it runs through the projector. The only give-away is that the lens is sticking out at least two feet lower than it would normally. We'll keep it covered until the lights go out.

We decide not to risk a trial run of the footage. We will keep it as pristine as possible, no scratches or damage of any kind. This means that all of us will see what I shot for the first time with our visitors. I am sick with worry. It could be a nightmare.

On the other hand, if we can pull off this screening and the footage is impressive, our financial concerns will be alleviated, and we may actually be able to pay ourselves for two months in a row.

The chief arrives with several council members, and we lead them downstairs, past the furnace, into what we have set up as a screening room.

All dressed up and looking very professional, we offer drinks and popcorn and shoot the breeze for a few minutes before taking our seats for the big presentation.

The chief makes a special point of greeting me. "Ruthie says hello," he declares with a twinkle.

"I hear you lost the bet," I kid him.

"Ya, so this better be good!"

The situation is so bizarre and amusing that I dare not look at any of the guys without risking a fit of the giggles. As our guests get seated, Mark and I slip behind the curtains ready to spin the reels. We flip off the light switch and uncover the lens.

Kenny has wired the room for sound, and the loud music begins. The sound of Santana makes an impressive introduction and covers the grinding sound of the metal reels as we begin to spin them backwards.

We have added a new Academy Leader to the head of the reels and the countdown blasts off, with great expectations. The first shots are very ragged, wobbling out of focus, searching for an image. Then everyone in the room is taken on a virtual roller-coaster ride with the music underscoring the sense of excitement and danger. I feel sick watching it, remembering my panic and inability to look through the lens. At first, I had just pointed the camera and hoped for the best.

Within a couple of minutes, the footage settles, and our guests are thrilled with the view. Everyone in the room is on the same plane, riding out the thrill of it all. I hear them oohing and ahhing together as we bank almost upside down, then soar up toward the sun, cutting through the clouds. There are places where my camera was pointing all over the place and I'm glad there is no sync sound as I remember that I was screaming, trying to communicate with the pilot who was truly testing my resolve and enjoying it.

Mark and I can't keep up spinning the reels; eventually the film starts spilling on the floor, thankfully out of sight. We manage the reel change with some finesse, while Dale breaks open a case of beer.

The final shots, taken from the ground, are boring in comparison to the aerials, and we turn down the music. Our guests begin to confer. The chief begins. "Well, that was something, wasn't it?" He turns in his seat, looking for me, "Where is that girl?"

I step out of the shadows.

"The pilot told us you threw up once or twice."

I nod sheepishly. "Ya. He did his best."

The chief chuckles. "He's a bad boy, that one, but you hung

in there. Surprised him." He turns to Dale. "Good thing you didn't tell me she was a girl. I might have put up a fuss."

He puts on his hat and stands up. "If you don't mind, I'd like to speak to my men a moment ... we'll go outside."

Dale shows them out, and the rest of us collapse where we are, sharing a mutual sigh of relief. "Other than it being upside down," I venture, "what did you think?"

"I'm surprised that your last night's supper wasn't in the shots," says Alan. "I had to close my eyes."

"Me too," says Reevan, "but every once in a while I took a gander and it was decent."

"Decent?" I ask.

"Way decent," interjects Rico, "and I'm glad it was you and not me." He smiles, we start to laugh. "Was that your foot that kept popping into the bottom of the frame?" he asks.

I nod, big-eyed. And they all crack up. "I was hanging from a makeshift harness made of belts. Holding onto the wing strut so tight, I could hardly let go when we landed. My hand was completely cramped up."

"Jesus, Wheeler ... what were you thinking?"

"I was thinking that it was maybe the last day of my life! But possibly the best. It was incredible up there."

They actually seem impressed with what I did ... I think I've earned a few brownie points here.

Dale comes back in, looking hopeful. "If they go for this, maybe we'll buy a flat-bed editing machine."

We all cheer, "Ya!"

"Wouldn't that make syncing rushes a slice!" I say, imagining that I will be back hand-cranking the reels soon enough.

We wait, not wanting to jinx ourselves with assurances.

"Guess I won't have to sell my car then, eh?" I venture.

"Nobody would buy it," says Kenny. "It's not a car, it's a key chain."

The door opens and it's the chief. He holds the moment, as we all stand up. "We're in," he says, stone-faced, then breaks into a smile. "We're going to make some movies!"

We all laugh and mutter words of joy. His men follow him in, and we all shake hands, sharing the mutual excitement.

"We'll be in touch. The funding is almost sewn up ... so we should know within a week. And we got a lawyer ... we'll get him together with Dale here, make it all legal like ..."

"Great," says Dale, "any time you're ready."

"Oh! And we're having some elders come in and tell all the old legends to the whole school in a couple of weeks ... some of them are getting kinda old, you know, so we thought, before they forget, we'd like to get them on film, before these stories are lost. What do you think of that?"

We all agree enthusiastically, truthfully. "It's a great idea!" "We can do that!" "We'll be there." "Let us know as soon as you can!"

Just as he's going out the door, he turns, "And oh, one last thing ..."

We all nod. He points at me, "We want her to shoot it!" He laughs at his own mischief. "She deserves it, don't you think?"

A FEW DAYS LATER I went to Dr. Smith and formally withdrew from my master's program. I had the privilege to do what my mother couldn't. I was single and free to choose my path, make mistakes, and risk being a failure.

Filmwest signed the deal with the Saddle Lake Reserve, and I shot their first educational film, named after one of their traditional stories, *Little Startlers*. This was the beginning of what has now become one of the most respected and forward-thinking First Nations educational systems in North America.

THE WOMAN WHO DIDN'T EXIST

Edmonton, 1973

CFRN RADIO INTERVIEW

ME: We never imagined that so many women would turn up! The article in the *Journal* simply said that we were going to make a film about what it would be like to be a woman who leaves a marriage without getting a divorce. We wanted to talk to anyone who had just walked out of her marriage and started all over.

INTERVIEWER: I see. So you advertised a time and place ...

ME: Yes, and when we arrived to open the doors, there was a lineup a block long. Young. Old. Rich. Poor. Fat. Thin. We should have had a camera rolling that day because they all had stories to tell.

INTERVIEWER: But. Ah.... Aren't you are a member of something called Filmwest? I know some of those guys.

ME: Yes, but they were not so interested in this project so I invited three women to join me and we applied for a grant. As you may know, 1975 will be International Women's Year!

INTERVIEWER: I didn't know that...

ME: ... and there is money available — for women like me, artists, choreographers.... Anyway — the goal was to train women to make films. I was like the expert, which was ludicrous because I have never made a film, but we did not know of a woman within a thousand miles who had. I'd worked on half a dozen short films, as an editor and a cameraman, I mean camerawoman (that's a mouthful, eh?), so I did know more than anyone, but that wasn't much. Only one other woman, Lorna, had even held a movie camera before —

INTERVIEWER: But you still got a grant? To make a film?

ME: Yes. I guess it was such a novel idea — women making movies about women — that we got the money!

INTERVIEWER: So, who is in your movie?

ME: Ha! One of the women who showed up that Saturday became our star. She was a natural. She just had to be herself. Beyond that, we called on our friends and relatives to take the other roles. Nobody got paid. There were no movie stars. No script, in fact. We took the stories we were told, boiled them down into one story (so many were similar), then broke the story into scenes, and blundered through shooting them, improvising as we went.

INTERVIEWER: That sounds tricky.

ME: Not really. Basically, we discovered that any woman who leaves a marriage has no rights. She can't open a bank account, or legitimately rent a place, get a loan, buy a car, get insurance, even go back to school — unless, of course, her father steps in and co-signs.

INTERVIEWER: Really. [*chuckling*] I'll make sure my wife knows that. [*pause*] But who did the camerawork and so on...?

ME: We did. That was the point.

INTERVIEWER: You did? Well! So the film is going to be shown on national television?

ME: Yes. A week from today. It's called *One Woman*. It will be on CBC at 4 p.m.

INTERVIEWER: Are you going to make another film?

ME: I hope so. I'm very interested in history from a female prospective. There is virtually nothing in the archives, or taught in our schools about women and what they have done. Lorna is going to continue working with me. We've found some fantastic material on the suffragettes.

INTERVIEWER: The what?

ME: The incredible women who fought to get the vote. In 1916. Women on the prairies were the first in Canada to be enfranchised, even though the Prairie provinces were the last to be settled.

INTERVIEWER: And why was that, do you suppose?

ME: That's what I want to find out! We are going to talk to and document the women who are still alive and remember those days — we are on a mission.

INTERVIEWER: Well best of luck with that. It's always a treat to have a young woman on the show with new ideas!

THOUGH LIFE IS FULL and I am busy, I can barely make the rent on my sixty dollars a month one-bedroom apartment. The Parkview is an old three-storey brick building, the lone survivor of a neighbourhood sacrificed for the new James Mac-Donald Bridge, which boasts six lanes. I have a wild assortment of furniture, most of it junk, some of it here when I moved in. Only my piano will leave with me when and if I ever move. The ceilings are high and the bathtub is painted pink and looks funky. The place is dusty, the walls are cracked, but I like it. My hours are out of whack; living alone suits me.

I barely hear the phone ring above the roar of morning traffic. Naked, I scramble to the kitchen and grab the phone off the wall. It must be early — there is just a faint glow of light in the winter morning sky.

"Hello!"

"Is this the young lady who was on the radio yesterday?" The raspy old voice is sweetened with an Irish lilt.

I clear my morning throat. "Yes, it is. Who is this, please?" I see that it is 6 a.m.

"My name is Mrs. Doris Ward and I listened to you. Would like you to come down and see me in Brooks?" The telephone reception is breaking up — she must be on a pay phone.

"Brooks? Where is that exactly?"

"About 103 miles southeast of Calgary."

"Oh! Well. Thank you for the invitation, Mrs. Ward, but that's a four- or five-hour drive away in this weather!" I respond politely. "What did you want to talk to me about?"

"You were wondering why women on the prairies were the first to get the vote. I was born in 1884, you see — I came to this country when I was 19. I saw it all."

"I am sure you have some stories to tell. But I'm just starting on this project — I haven't done the research or raised any money yet. Perhaps in the spring —"

"I am almost ninety years old, Miss Wheeler. You'll not be wanting to put me off 'til spring. I could be pushing up daisies by then. I want you to come down now while I still have my wits about me."

"Were you involved in the suffrage movement?"

"Yes and no. I was there … of course. And I can tell you why we got the vote first. Will you come?"

"Yes, but the thing is," I reply, "I would like the interview to be on camera —"

"Don't be ridiculous. I don't want my picture taken! If you want research, I'm it. If you want history … I am history. Most of us originals are dead now — only a few of us left. You get on down here."

She has a point. Most women her age have forgotten a lot, or are too shy to say much. This woman sounds forthright and spunky. "Alright, Mrs. Ward. I'm coming down to see you."

"When?"

"I'll need to borrow a car. Maybe Wednesday."

"What time?"

"I should be there around two o'clock."

"Thank you very much." Her voice is softened by emotion. "I live in the seniors' lodge, right on the highway as you come into town. Low building with a big parking lot. It's not much to look at. Flat roof. Easily missed."

"I'll find it," I assure her.

"We'll have tea," she adds.

IT'S A BAD DAY to be driving across the flatlands, with harsh winter winds blowing in from the northwest. Unfortunately, I couldn't talk anyone out of a car, so I'm being tossed around in my tiny Fiat. Even with new tires, it's barely hanging onto the icy road as 18-wheelers thunder past me in both directions, sucking me sideways, kicking up icy slush that plasters my windshield and renders me momentarily blind. It's almost three when I finally see the grain elevators of Brooks, silhouetted against the distant horizon.

Thankfully, the parking lot has power outlets, which means I can plug in my block heater so my little car will start when I'm ready to leave. The bitter sting of the wind cuts into my skin and my throat stings as I slog through the salted, mushy snow toward the front door.

Inside, the air is hot and stale. The green linoleum floor in the hallway is worn down in the middle, revealing a previous layer of speckled beige. A sign on the windowless wall directs me to the office where a woman, who has clearly been expecting me, tells me that Mrs. Ward is waiting for me in the dining hall.

The tiny woman is in a wheelchair, sitting next to a table by a window. A china teapot and matching cups and saucers stand ready. She must have watched for me to arrive. Holding out her hand, she welcomes me, "Miss Wheeler? I thought you might have changed your mind, with the weather getting worse."

I take both her hands in mine. "No, no, I'm from good prairie stock, Mrs. Ward. Bad weather just makes for good conversation."

"Well, we have lots to talk about! Were the roads bad?"

"Yes, I had to go more slowly. But it's good to meet you." Her fingers are bony and cold, but her grip still has conviction.

"My! Your hands are so warm! Mine are never warm."

"Cold hands, warm heart," I offer.

"Not true," she jokes. "My heart can be as cold as a witch's tit."

I chuckle, surprised by her choice of words. She lacks the formality I would expect from an older woman. I pull up a chair as she pours two cups of tea.

"This might be a little bitter and not so hot. Help yourself to the stale cookies." She smiles. "I asked them not to disturb us. There are a lot of nosy ninnies sniffing about in this place. They'll be wondering who you are. Ha! I thought this would be the best place, while everyone is having their nap."

"It's perfect," I reassure her.

She is wearing a sweet home-sewn blue dress, with matching barrettes in her hair that give her a girlish look. Her eyes are still fired up and her grey hair holds a hint of natural red.

"The receptionist at the radio station was reluctant to give me your phone number, but I insisted. I would have written to you, but I'm not much of a writer anymore. My handwriting is such a scrawl now — I can't read it myself!" She shrugs. "I used to be proud of my writing!"

Her tea pouring is a little shaky so I take over. "Well, I'm anxious to hear your story, Mrs. Ward." I get out my notepad and select a cookie from the paper plate. I should've brought something for tea. Where are my manners? "Just talk to me like I'm your granddaughter, wanting to know what it was like for you."

"Oh, well, I hope you are more interested than they are!" I can see she can be a bit of a grump.

I ignore her complaint as I, too, have not shown much interest in my own grandmother's past until recently. Unfortunately, she died when I was still a brat. "Tell me where you're from and how you got to Canada. I'm here to listen," I say, with a bit too much enthusiasm.

"Well, I was the youngest of eleven. My father died when I was six, my mom when I was twelve. We lived in the tenements, in Dublin. So I was just a kid when I went to work in the factories. That's the way it was then — most people didn't live past fifty. I never expected to live this long! It's not for everyone, I can tell you that!" She makes a funny old face and laughs at my reaction.

"But here you are! However did you get here?" I don't need to encourage her — she's obviously itching to tell her story. She even has her old diary at hand, in case she wants to look up a detail or two.

"Well, that's a short question ... with a long answer. So here I go!

"I WAS EIGHTEEN, yes, and I should have been married, I could have been married, but I didn't want my life to begin and end up in the same stinking place. What would be the point of that? I wanted to see the world.

"There was a lot of talk at the time about the New World, with posters showing how you could start a new life in Canada by homesteading — assuming you were a man, of course. Luckily, I could read and write. The first girl in my extended family to do so. My brother taught me, and, glory be, one day I was at the church and I saw — on the pin board — an advertisement from a man in Alberta who wanted a wife! I confess I tore the note down before anyone else could see it. Ha! It said that he owned an enormous piece of land that included a lake and a solid house. He had cattle and pigs and a barn and a well — it sounded just wonderful. He wanted a woman who could read and write, but wasn't afraid of hard work.

"I thought to myself, well, here is an educated gentleman — with high expectations. I'll be lucky to land him. So I replied with a formal letter of inquiry, trying to sound above my station and not too eager. Six weeks later, I got a response! Oh my, I was so encouraged. His name was Matthew Ward. His letter was impressive, his handwriting neat, and his language refined. Back and forth we wrote for more than a year, it taking a full two months for a letter to be sent and delivered. He asked if I could cook, and sew, and garden, if I was good with animals — and of course, 'did I want a large family?' Well, in those days, there was no choice of whether you had children or not. And I certainly wanted a family of my own.

"Then he asked for a photograph, which was a huge expense for me. The picture was good though — I was surprised when I saw it. I have it here to show you."

She opens her sewing bag. Inside, carefully wrapped in an embroidered cloth, is the photo. Beautifully hand-tinted, it reveals a stunning young woman, wearing a heavy woollen dress and shawl, staring straight at the lens. She is strong and confident, with big, wide eyes fringed with long lashes. Her thick red flowing hair is pulled back in waves, tied in ribbon.

"My goodness, Mrs. Ward! You were a showstopper," I tease. "He must have been very pleased to see such a beauty!"

"Yes," she giggles. "It was the first time I'd ever seen myself, with no mirror of my own. I knew I had good teeth and hair, but nobody had told me, Doris dear, you are a fine-looking woman! I guess I always had my head down, hair wrapped in a scarf, trying not to be noticed. Too many of my friends had started their marriages with a bun in the oven, and I swore that my life would be different from theirs. And this was my chance."

"So when Mr. Ward got the picture, I presume he agreed that you would suit him just fine."

She carefully puts the picture back in the box and continues.

"Yes, he liked what he saw. In good order, he sent me the money for passage. I sailed from Cork, knowing I would never be back. And it was awful, a bloody awful boat. I was in the cursed bottom, wet and mucky the whole time."

"Seasick?"

"Oh yes. We all were. Miserable. But I did have some admirers on the boat, oh yes. One young fellow snuck me up to first class — even proposed marriage! There were far more men than women, of course — but I didn't alter my course. I was going to marry Matthew Ward, have a big family, and prosper in the New World! Ha!" She shakes her head, acknowledging the irony, unable to hide some bitterness.

"So, then you landed in Halifax, and took a train across the country?"

"Yes. What a long but glorious journey that was — the country, so new and untouched. I loved it. It took almost a week. By the time I reached Calgary, I had heard enough to give me pause. One couple that got on in Manitoba had decided to quit after two years of hardship. Such a sad pair they were, having lost two children. They advised me to turn around and go straight back home. Others were heading further west, across the mountains to the coast where the weather was not so harsh. There were several sweet young men amongst them ... I could have joined them, but no. When we pulled into the Calgary station, I got off."

"And what was Cowtown Calgary like in those days?" I ask.

"It didn't look too bad. Actually, quite beautiful. You could see to the mountains that day ... but the mud! Mixed in with the manure! Oh my."

"And was he there?"

"Oh yes, he was there, waiting with a horse and wagon full of provisions. I heard him calling out my name, and then I saw him as he pushed through the crowd to get to me. I should have known then that he was not a true gentleman, as he embraced me long and hard, right in front of everybody, pushing himself against me, holding me in a way that was — too familiar.

"I'd never been hugged like that before ... by a man. But I managed to convince myself that his behaviour was exceptional. He had waited a long time for my arrival and was overcome with anticipation. My bigger complaint was that he was filthy. His hair was stiff with sweat and dust, combed right back. He had dressed up some, his clothes looked new, but he smelled like — a slop pail left too long."

The disgusting memory stops her momentarily. She takes a sip of her tea.

"Had you seen a picture of him?" I ask.

She shakes her head. "No, I had not. He was a lot older than I imagined, close to forty, I guessed ... tall and very thin. Truthfully, I was disappointed. He saw it in my face. I was sorry I could not conceal my reaction, but no matter. He had not made much of an effort and I was put off."

"You must have thought of running."

"I would've. But he took me directly to the church and he paid the minister flat out to marry us right there and then. The minister was annoyed by Matthew's impatience and his stench. He asked me directly if I was sure I had given my consent enough thought. Even he could not believe that I had chosen to marry this man.

"What could I do? No money. No options. I had given my word and he'd paid for my ticket. I reassured the minister that I was doing this willingly. So then he insisted that Matthew and I go to the local rest house where we could have a meal as well as a bath."

"Good for him! You must have been relieved —"

"It annoyed Matthew who said it was 'a waste of time and money,' but I was thankful. I didn't smell like a spring rose either, having been in the same clothes for weeks. And, once Matthew dressed up, he was a handsome man in a wild kind of way — a bit wolfish, but nevertheless fit."

"So you went back to the church that day?"

"And again, the minister was uneasy, asking me questions I couldn't answer. I didn't know where we were going. I didn't even know Matthew's middle name. He offered us a room, and again suggested that I could do better. 'If I were so lucky to find such a fine wife, I'd be sure she was rested and content after such a long journey,' he said, implying for certain that he was single!

"He was a good-looking younger man. That he was. And Matthew saw that he was tempting me. He got angry, frightening actually, and demanded that we begin the proceedings immediately. So we did.

"I have imagined a million times what would have happened if I had refused Matthew that day. But it was beyond my imagination then. The plan had been set. After the brief ceremony, even though the sun was going down, we headed out of the city."

"Knowing he was a difficult man ..."

"Not just difficult. He was insanely jealous, possessive. Unpredictable. Possibly dangerous. He was more than one person really. He could be reasonable, and smart, even charming ... singing like the world was his kingdom and dancing funny, making me laugh, when boom! — his mood would shift. Suddenly, he'd be crying, 'The whole world is against me. The house will never be built. It's all too much work. I hate everybody. Can't trust anybody — especially you!' Then the next day, he'd be back again, dreaming of the house he was going to build."

"How far were you from Calgary?"

"It was a two-day walk. About sixty miles. We didn't get very far that first night. I asked a lot of questions, but he was in his own head, pouting. After a couple of hours, we stopped. I was terrified. Not just of him but of what might be out there in the wild. I'd never lived in the country. I was used to the city — buildings, noise, and people. He made a fire and I started a meal. He stopped working and watched me for a time. Then, out of the blue, he said, 'Take off your clothes!' Just like that! 'Take them off! I want to see what I got.'"

The memory embarrasses her even now, and she fusses with her buttons. I try to catch up with my notes and give her a minute to flush out the humiliation she still feels.

"I had never been with a man, never seen a man naked," she confesses. "I knew that in marriage I would have to let him 'satisfy himself,' but it wasn't clear to me what that meant. Nothing had ever been explained to me, in plain English. I assumed that it would come naturally, that it would be romantic and sweet.

"At first I refused, but the more I fought him, the more excited he became. I broke away and ran into the darkness, into the bush — but I stumbled and he fell upon me. When he started to tear at my new blouse, I became very angry. I yelled at him to stop — I'd do what he wanted. It was going to happen anyway. And nobody would know. Nobody would care. Anything I did would make it worse. So I succumbed and went limp.

"It was awkward and unpleasant. Mercifully, he made quick work of it and was pleased with himself. He took out his harmonica and started to play while I cooked. And I thought, 'Well maybe that's it then. We just had to get that over with and now we can get on.'" She goes quiet, and takes a sip of tea, like she is trying to swallow the anger that keeps bubbling up.

"I'm sorry you had to go through that," I mutter, feeling ineffective.

"Oh, that was just the beginning," she says in a hushed voice. "Forgive me for being so indiscreet, but I remember it ever so vividly."

"Please take your time...."

She poured more tea. "I know, people talk about 'the settlers, the salt of the earth, the hard-working, God-fearing, honest and loving people' like you see on television, on *Bonanza* — but the truth is, many of us were out in the middle of bloody nowhere, unprotected, living a nightmare. The nice ladies with comfortable parlours were having tea, talking about getting the vote — for themselves and other nice ladies.

"History, Miss Wheeler, is always about the successful and the charming folks who have their pictures in the paper. History is what people want to remember, when it should be about what we shouldn't forget. Many settlers were shattered by the experience. Broken. Matthew was already cracked when I met him.

"So, that first night he had his way with me over and over, like a cat with an injured mouse. When he was finished with me, I tried to get away, but he caught me and tied me up. I was bruised from head to foot, and covered with the smell of him. In the morning, he put me in the back of the wagon — but I managed to bite him hard. Infuriated that I had hurt him, he whipped the poor horse all the way home, as though now it was her fault. We were less than two days wed, and both of us were in a rage.

"The following afternoon, we pulled up to his godforsaken place. A herd of bony cattle rambled toward us, hoping to be fed. There was no house, no barn. A wee granary was tucked away in the soggy bushes, maybe eight by ten feet but no more. And this shack was to be my home."

"Oh no!" I groan.

"Well, it was never a home — it was more like a cage, a place to keep me locked up so I wouldn't run away. Inside, there was a wee stove, a straw bed on the floor, and a trunk that served as a table, pushed up against the wall. It was worse than a barn really, with no windows, no place to wash up, only a bucket. There wasn't even a well, just a slough in the summer and melted snow in the winter.

"I learned that the way to stay safe was to please him in every way I could. I had to be smart because, even though he was a bit loony, he was not dim-witted. In fact, he was very clever. For instance, he planned every detail of this house he was going to build, the biggest and best house you could imagine, placed precisely on a hill according to which way the wind would blow in the coldest of times ... and where the sun would be each month of the year, with windows taking full advantage of the view. He wanted to see the sun come up in the morning through the kitchen windows. And there would be a grand, deep porch on the west side so he could sit and watch it set. Even I took pleasure in imagining how grand it would be.

"I worked hard, not just gardening and cooking, but also in the fields. I became his beast of burden, clearing the land, pulling out stumps, gathering large rocks for the foundation of this magnificent house.

"And yes, there were moments of wonder. The land, so untamed, so changeable, gave me a sense of being at one with the universe, with God. I loved to watch the night sky as it rotated perfectly every night. Matthew knew all the constellations and changes in the moon; I learned a lot from him. But he would never let me out of his sight."

"What about neighbours?" I ask.

"We had no neighbours. Sometimes I saw smoke rising from far away. You see, there were no roads yet. In fact, you had to cross a good-sized creek to get to our place. No one knew I was there, of course, except for some Indians maybe. I never saw them. Matthew told me they were very danger-ous, so I always stayed out of sight and had a gun near me. Of course, that was just another one of Matthew's games to keep me put.

"In the summer, Matthew went to town on Saturdays —

leaving me locked up in the shack. Usually he came back all cleaned up and cheerful. I didn't ask any questions about what he did or whom he saw. I was glad enough to be left alone.

"We harvested ten acres the first year — finishing just before winter set in. He was caught up hunting and butchering, while I filled the cellar, which we had dug into the side of the hill, with root vegetables for the winter.

"By November, I knew I was pregnant. When I told him, he was thrilled, assuming it was a boy of course. I didn't mind. Suddenly I was precious, carrying his wee prince. He went to town and bought a large tub for bathing, and ordered in a bed. I was convinced that the worst was over. Life would keep getting better and better.

"Trouble was, neither of us knew anything about making babies — how long it took, or what to do when the baby came. Matthew knew that a dog took two months, a sheep four, a horse eleven. Our logic was that a human would take longer. Can you imagine?"

"Was there a doctor in town, or a midwife?"

"Well, I didn't know of one, of course. He planned to go into town before Christmas and I begged him to take me with him, so I might talk to another woman about what was happening. How should I prepare? What should I expect? I was huge and could feel the baby moving inside of me. But he kept saying that we didn't need anyone; that the birth would take care of itself. He wasn't going to bring someone out here for something that should come natural.

"He left for town, with me locked up as usual, so I wouldn't 'do anything foolish.' Later that day, it started to snow. I got a fire going and could hear the storm blowing outside. I figured that I would be locked up for a long time if the weather got worse and he couldn't get back. The cows came in close, looking for shelter.

"It was a surprise to me, when suddenly my clothing was wet and a sharp pain brought me to my knees. For a time, I lay on the floor, thinking it would happen quickly. But it didn't, and I started to get cold and weak. I got out of my wet clothes, and put all of the blankets and rags I had onto the bed.

"The fire went out, but I could not fix it. For hours, I was in labour, until the pains came one after the other, as they do, and I lost control. I called out for mercy. I thought I was going to die.

"Finally, I felt the baby's head, pushing through me and out. I was so tired, I could hardly muster any strength. I felt the release of its shoulders and a gush of fluids. Once I got my breath, I reached down and pulled the baby free from my body. It was limp and blue and I thought it was dead. I gave it a little shake and its dark little eyes opened and looked straight into mine. It was like this wee soul had miraculously arrived from the unknown, to give me strength. I will never forget that moment. Ever. It was the last thing that happened before I passed out.

"Matthew got home and found us there, wrapped up together, under the mess of blankets. I woke up with him pulling them back, pushing me away and trying to get a look. The baby started to cry. 'A goddamned girl.' That's what he said. 'A goddamned girl!'

"He didn't want to have anything to do with her. Or me. He did cut the cord and took the 'stinking mess,' as he called it, out to the pig. I'm sure the pig was happy about that, but I thought it was a wicked thing to do.

"When he came back inside, he was morose and started to drink. I got up, made a fire, cleaned myself up as best I could, and then went back to bed."

"And the baby?"

"Margaret was her name, but she was called Maggie right from the start. She was perfect in every way, and began to suck eagerly once she got a taste of my juice. I couldn't take my eyes off of her — amazed that I had brought this darling dear dolly into the world. I wanted to tell someone, to show her off, you know? But I had no one to tell. I had written a letter to my brother, but nothing came back. In a way, the baby and I didn't exist. At night, I would lie in the dark and think — there must be other women like me, all over the world. Alone and forgotten."

"I don't know how you could bear it, boxed up in that cold dark place, in the winter. I would have gone mad."

"Aye. We rarely spoke. The snow was constant. He didn't talk to me, but he talked to the Almighty constantly. And he was convinced that he was one of God's chosen — that he could hear God's voice inside his head and that he could read my mind. Ha! It wasn't too hard to read my mind. I had but one thought and that was 'How can I get away from him?'"

"Did he ... hit you?"

"Oh ... yes. Like I was just another animal — he smacked me as a matter of course, whenever he was displeased. That was a given. I confess I might have thought of doing him some harm, while he was sleeping, given the circumstances. Oh yes ... I thought about that a lot. But a wounded bear is more dangerous than a sleeping bear. I decided that my kitchen knife was not long enough." She laughs bitterly at the memory.

"But then, one day, soon after he'd gotten back from his usual trip to town, I found a penny in the lining of his coat. I hid it in my rags. A few weeks later, I found a nickel in the wagon, caught between the floorboards. I saw him counting his money. He knew he was short, and I watched him looking all over, confused. He accused me of stealing, but I played dumb. I figured I would need at least three dollars, a lot of money at the time, to get myself and the baby on a train and away.

"I tried to be patient, but by midsummer I was pregnant again. With a hopeful heart, Matthew added a shed to the shack so we'd have room for a crib. The child came in February. It was another girl. Again, I delivered it alone and thought I was going to die. But I didn't. I was better prepared and tougher this time. I had a better sense of what had to be done and it was easier.

"I was his slave now, for I would do anything to protect my babies. He made ridiculous demands — some of them disgusting. He resented having to provide for the three of us. I was losing weight and feeling weak, but still he was determined to have a son.

"We were living on so little that I didn't think I would survive another delivery on my own. So — I hope you don't find this offensive — I started to stuff myself down there with rags. Rags soaked in different things, like rhubarb juice, lye soap, or vinegar. Something must have worked because the babies stopped coming. He wouldn't leave me alone, but I didn't get pregnant.

"Then, one spring night, when I saw he was sleeping deeply, I put my long-time plan into action. I took the key from his pocket and opened his trunk. I took three dollars from his money box and added it to the forty-two cents I had gathered.

"Maggie was four and a half, and Brigitt was three. Both of them were able to walk some distance on their own, and both were perfectly aware that we were sneaking away from their father."

"But you didn't know where you were!"

"No. But anywhere away would be better. With a sense of delight, I blocked the door from the outside. Then I opened the corrals and let all the animals go, including the horse. They charged out into the fields and away. I figured Mathew would go after them before he came after us. Maybe he would be glad to see us gone.

"Using the North Star to guide me, we headed south. We didn't follow any paths and the children didn't have proper shoes, so the going was slow. But sure enough, after hours of slogging through fields of mud and climbing over deadwood in the aspen forests, I saw something in the distance that made me weep. I saw a steeple, flashing like a beacon, reflecting the light of the morning sun. What a bedazzling sight that was. We arrived at the small wooden church on the edge of town. The doors were open but nobody was inside, so I told the girls to go lie down on the pew and rest, while I went next door to the rectory.

"As I crossed the small graveyard outside the church, I could see the road to town and the railway crossing over it. There must be a station, I told myself. With a little help, I would be on the next train. In front of the rectory, there were two lovely lilac bushes in full bloom. I remember the perfume, the sweetness of spring. It gave me hope. I gave the door a good strong knock and immediately a cheerful voice called out from inside, 'Hello! Come in!' It was a woman!

"It had been years since I had talked to a woman. What would she think of me, standing out here stinking up her yard? Haggard and filthy, with my hair pulled back into a mangy knot, I couldn't imagine she would want me inside her house.

"The voice kept chirping away at me, 'I'll be right there, make yourself at home,' she went on, but I didn't presume to go in. Finally, the door opened, and a short, round woman stood there looking at me. Everything she wore was clean and crisp and ironed. Her hair was braided and coiled perfectly on the nape of her neck. She scanned my frightened face, then gracefully reacted. 'Oh my, you poor soul,' she said. 'What have you got on your feet? Where are your boots? Come in and get warmed up, my dear.'"

Doris's voice breaks as she remembers this first meeting and I can't help but weep along with her. She blows her nose and continues. "Her voice was soft and loving, genuine. When I could finally speak, I told her that my two wee girls were waiting in the church, needing to be fed. Without hesitation, she came with me to get them. Seeing their pale frightened faces, she was overcome with pity and tried to gather them up in her ample arms, but they were shy and backed away."

"What was her name?" I ask.

"Peggy, aye, Peggy. She led us to the back to her kitchen and wrapped my girls, with such care, in blankets, and sat them down in front of her big, beautiful stove. Her house was shining. There was fresh baking on the counter and soup stock bubbling on the stove.

"I told her straight out that we were trying to escape, that I had a wee bit of money. Did she know when the next train out of here would come? 'Tomorrow at noon,' she told me while she set the table and put out some warm bread and left-over chicken. She told us her husband was in town helping some folks move. 'You have something to eat and I'll be back soon,' she said. I'm glad she left us alone, because this was the first time my girls had actually sat at a table like civilized people. They had no idea what to do with the knives and forks, napkins and saltshakers.

"When Reverend Ruttledge arrived, in his long tailored coat, he took off his hat and had a good long look at us. Then he suggested to his missus that she should give the girls a bath. The girls followed her to the bathhouse across the yard, and the two of us were left alone.

"'My wife told me you are unhappy,' he said, 'that it's been very difficult for you. I see that. I'll go with you out to the farm tomorrow, and speak to your husband.'

"Horrified, I exploded with defiance. 'No sir. I am not going back there! Never. We've been living like animals — can't you see that? My babies are starving. My husband is a monster!' He kept nodding but remained unmoved as I raged on. At some point, I was completely spent and collapsed on the floor. He kept his distance, but asked, 'What is your name, Madame?'

"'Doris Ward,' I said. That seemed to shake him; I could see it immediately. Then he asked me what was my husband's name. 'Matthew Ward,' I told him.

"That changed everything. He was thunderstruck by my answer and sat down. 'Matthew Ward?' He kept repeating it over and over. 'Are those his children then, those two girls?' he asked.

"'Yes,' I said, 'though he doesn't seem to want them. He doesn't even call them by name. He only wants a boy.' Now that I had his attention, I started all over. 'Please sir,' I begged, 'send us away somewhere safe. If he finds us here, he will kill us all.'

"'How long have you been married?' he asked, like he still couldn't believe it.

"I told him, 'About five years, sir. I don't know what date it is now, but I arrived in Calgary on April 29, 1903.'

"Looking me straight in the eye, he said, 'I wish I had known, Mrs. Ward. This has been going on much too long.' With that, he got up and left.

"Peggy came back with the girls all cleaned up, wearing borrowed nighties that were white, real white. I had not seen white for a while. And their hair was carefully braided. They looked so sweet. Peggy seemed anxious. Different. She said that the Reverend thought it was best for us to stay with them for the night. Then she prepared a lovely fresh bath for me and gave us all clean clothes and shoes, which had been sent out from another Presbyterian congregation in Toronto.

"What a mess I was! Unused to this kindness, I could hardly keep my emotions under control. She told me that her deepest regret was that she had no children of her own, but she made up for it by being charitable. We had a fine meal of stew with meat and vegetables. Freshly harvested and stewed rhubarb with cream. Then she put us to bed in her parlour, which was so warm and cozy. The walls were covered with beautiful paintings, and there were shelves full of books. Oh my, I thought to myself, if we could stay here forever, I would die happy!"

Doris pours herself another cup of tea. I've hardly touched mine; she has me spellbound with her Irish lilt and her harrowing story. The woman at the desk crosses the hall, comes toward us, and asks how long we're going to be. "We've got to set the tables for dinner soon," she says. Impatiently, Doris shoots back at her, "Not for another bloody hour, Gladys. I know that. Mind your own business."

The woman doesn't know quite what to say. She looks me over, assessing the situation. "Don't mind her language," she says to me. "She's one egg short of a dozen."

"Oh, I don't mind her bloody language one bit," I retort, and the woman leaves, miffed. Doris and I share a moment of amusement.

"I think you and I are cut from the same cloth, dear," she says to me.

"Yes, I think we are. Go on," I urge her, "before she comes back and chases us out with a fork." She giggles.

"Well, the Reverend left the house in the morning before I could speak to him. I asked Peggy what she thought he would do for us. She simply said, 'I've put a lunch together for you. For the train. I think we should go down there early. Now.'

"She pulled a cookie jar down from a cupboard and took out ten one-dollar bills. 'I hope this will help,' she said. 'Just take it please, make no fuss.'

"'Thank you so much. One day I'll pay you back. I promise.'

"We were hurrying down the lane when I could feel a pounding in my head. Something tried to warn me — a shift in the wind, a vibration perhaps, the sound of the trotting horse. Maybe it was the smell of him or some wild instinct. But I knew he was there before I saw him riding up with the Reverend. I froze.

"There was a fury in his eyes as he jumped off the wagon and came rushing toward me. I picked up Brigitt and tried to run, but it was hopeless. He grabbed me by the arm, and yanked the two of us toward the wagon. I reached out to Peggy. 'Help me,' I begged. 'We can't go back!'

"She turned to her husband and addressed him by his first name, 'Michael — please!' He put his hand up, commanding

119

her to keep her mouth shut, and with a calm 'godly' voice, told her, 'Go inside, Peggy. Make a pot of tea.' Without looking at me, she turned and hurried away.

"Matthew threw Brigitt and me in the wagon, but Maggie took off, knowing he was strong but not fast enough to catch her and she disappeared into the brush. He was fuming. 'Get back here, you little bugger, or I'll squeeze your eyes out! You hear me? Afraid of the dark, are you? You'll never see light again!' I remember those exact words.

"The Reverend was visibly shocked by this beastly outburst and finally intervened. 'Matthew!' he commanded, as if he were talking to a naughty child. 'Contain yourself! I know you were worried, but calm down. You have your wife back,' he said, 'and your girl will change her mind. She'll come back. Get a hold of yourself! Be a man.' He went on like that.

"I was surprised to see that Matthew was listening, though he was huffing and puffing, struggling to get his temper under control. We all stood there, not knowing what was coming next. It felt like Matthew could blow at any moment, but the Reverend kept talking. 'You are a lucky man. What more could you ask for? They are safe and sound. You have been blessed by the Lord with a beautiful wife and two healthy children. Be grateful, Matthew. You have a family.'

"No one dared to speak. Matthew shook his head violently, like he was trying to rid himself of his thoughts. I'd seen it before when he was wrestling with his demons. Then he spoke in a different tone. 'Yes, Reverend, they are safe. Thanks to you, sir.'

"'They were just lost, Matthew, is all. Isn't that right, Mrs. Ward?' The Reverend nodded at me to take up his efforts. I knew what he wanted me to say.

"'That's right,' I answered, gagging on the words, 'We got lost, is all.' Of course, that didn't explain why the animals were gone, why I had locked him in the shack — but it was enough to save face and it worked.

"The Reverend resumed his ploy, 'Why don't you bring your flock to church, Matthew, when you come next Sunday? Everyone would like to meet them.' Matthew was still struggling, but less vehemently.

"So now I understood where Matthew went on Saturdays, but, of course they were Sundays, not Saturdays. I had just lost track of the days. It was his chance to come into town, get cleaned up, and visit the people who believed he was an honest God-fearing man. I wondered what had he told the Reverend today on their ride into town.

"The men started walking toward the house, so Brigitt and I climbed out of the wagon, brushing off our new clothes, wanting to stay clean.

"Like a good boy, Matthew turned to me, contritely, 'I know you don't know better, Doris, and I apologize if I am impatient. But when you run off like that, I'm afraid for your life.' Then he turned to the Reverend, 'As I told you, she thinks nonsense sometimes. The life out there has been hard on her. She hasn't been wanting to meet anyone. She imagines things — hides things.'

"The Reverend patted him on the back. 'She needs you to be strong, Matthew. She's not the first to lose her bearings ... women need to feel safe.'

"I could see Maggie watching all this from a distance. Brigitt hung onto me, shaking. None of us felt safe.

"Somehow, we ended up in the parlour, all of us praying for our family to be together forever. Then I helped Peggy make some lunch and tried again to make my situation clear to her. I showed her my scars, my hands that were bent and worn from working, fingers broken from his beatings.

"Unfortunately, the Reverend came in and possibly heard some of — at any rate, he put his foot down. 'You must accept your lot in life, Mrs. Ward. You're only making things worse for yourself and your children. You are a mother and a wife, and your place is at home. Make the best of it.'

"At lunch, Peggy suggested that Maggie should be starting school soon, and perhaps a member of their congregation could board her in the fall. I grabbed onto the idea. 'She is a very helpful girl and she's smart. She deserves to go to school,' I said.

"'Every child deserves to go to school,' Peggy replied, 'and please, call me Peggy.' I felt as though we had a quiet understanding.

"When we came out, Maggie was waiting in the back of the wagon with her head down, hugging her knees, expecting the worst. But nobody mentioned her absence.

"The men hopped on board, with Matthew riding up front with the Reverend, who asked him, 'Do you have an order waiting down at the store, Matthew? Your wife might like to see the town, to get some supplies.'

"Matthew shook his head with regret and spoke confidentially. 'No sir. I don't trust her quite yet. She's apt to take what isn't hers.' That's what he said. And I guess the Reverend believed him.

"Peggy had given me a book about homesteading. As we bumped along, I opened it out of curiosity. She had signed her name on the front cover and had pinned some useful notes and recipes between the pages. I immediately recognized the handwriting! It was she who had written the letters I got from Matthew while I was still in Dublin! I had long suspected that he could not write at all — and here was proof of it.

"But now, the Reverend was convinced that I was a simpleton and a thief, and poor Matthew had been burdened by my lack of skills. Oh, I was angry at the injustice, but I stayed quiet, holding my kiddies, listening to the two men gabbing away. The Reverend suggested that Matthew should be satisfied with two children — for now — that he should get a house built before having more. But Matthew was firm. 'I want a son. I need a son, Reverend. Nothing sinful about that, is there?' The pastor had to admit that every man wanted a son.

"After that, things settled down a little, and I did all that was asked of me. Matthew gained weight and seemed content. On Sundays, we went to church and people were friendly, though we were a strange crew. Matthew had told the girls that he'd cut out their tongues if either of them complained to anyone, so they remained mute. I too kept my eyes down, careful not to draw attention to myself. We all appeared to be idiots, incapable of speaking a full sentence, but I got a sweet nod from Peggy every Sunday, which meant everything to me.

"And that's how we lived, for almost a year until, glory be, one of the families in town offered to take Maggie in, so she could go to school. To Matthew, this sounded like a dangerous proposition, but he couldn't refuse such generosity, knowing that the Ruttledges were involved.

"So that September, Peggy came to pick Maggie up. I remember seeing her in the distance, driving her buggy up the trail. Matthew marched out, wanting to stop her at the gate, but she drove right past him, giving him a friendly wave as though she had no idea that she was supposed to halt on command. I came out the door with the girls. Maggie had packed up her few things in a sack and was eager to get away.

"Peggy pulled up in front of the shack, and I watched her take a good look around. No barn. A pile of rocks. A couple of skinny cows and a horse that limped. Then she saw the small shack, worthy of goats perhaps, with a large door that only bolted from the outside. It was as I had described it, and now she knew for sure. I wondered if the Reverend had described it in a different way. Perhaps he didn't think she'd come out here on her own.

"I was standing there wearing the dress she gave me, now shredded by work — I had nothing else to wear. I asked her if she'd like some tea but she only shook her head — it was then that I saw that she was quietly weeping. I thanked her for the book, for her notes, and of course for the opportunity she was giving my Maggie.

"Matthew was watching us closely, so we kept our conversation sparse and unemotional. She gave me a parcel of cloth, some sugar, flour, and dried fruit. And, bless her soul, she gave me a lilac bush to plant. It's still alive; I go there and visit it every spring.

"We gave each other a brief hug and a long look of understanding. 'Doris, I must be off. The days are so short and I don't like travelling in the dark, but I'll see you at church.' To Matthew, she merely said, 'Good Day, Mr. Ward. You're looking well.' He nodded and said nothing.

"Maggie climbed into the back of the wagon, and Peggy told her to 'come up front.' That pleased my girl very much, and it pleased me too. My daughter was riding out of here, with dignity, not thrown in the back of the wagon like some loose cargo. Maggie knew she had to be careful. If anything she did or said caused Matthew any grief, he would take it out on her sister or me. I would miss my Maggie. She was a big help to me, but I was thrilled to see her escape this harsh life.

"Things changed after that. The fact that the Reverend's wife had denied Matthew's authority and had seen the way we lived in squalor may have had something to do with it, though nobody came to see us. Matthew refused to go to church and rarely went to town. I felt stranded and prayed that Maggie was safe and happy. We didn't see her until Christmas, when school closed for three weeks. Matthew went in early to fetch her. Peggy sent some parcels back with her, some extra blankets and food. She sent gifts, too, including tobacco for Matthew, which surprised him. I suspected he missed his visits with the Reverend; this was an invitation to resume the friendship, a reassurance perhaps that she had not closed the door on him.

"I got some garden seeds and some wool and a book by Nellie McClung called *Sowing Seeds in Danny*. There was a message on page twenty-five, written on the inside margin. 'Your Maggie is doing well at school. I think of you often. The only thing for certain is change. Do not despair.'

"It was as though she knew I was pregnant again. I didn't even tell Matthew, in hopes that one way or another it would end itself. I know that is sinful, but when spring came I threw myself into the work, trying to overdo it. We put in five more acres. I was sick with fatigue and the pregnancy. I started to show, but wore loose clothing. My stomach was bulging and my back ached.

"By the end of May, Matthew realized that a baby was on the way and was convinced he could will it to be a boy. He decided to go to church and give thanks ... as though our lack of prayer had resulted in two girls. We arrived early so he could boast to everyone that we had put in twenty-five acres total this year and his house was taking shape.

"He was so full of himself that Maggie didn't want to sit with us. She had become a working member of her adoptive family. They had given her a new printed dress and a spring hat adorned with flowers, which made her feel special. Her teacher made a point of telling us that Maggie was the smartest girl in her class. I was so proud of her and swallowed her rejection of us with a breath of relief. She looked healthy and happy — and as Matthew blathered on, she turned to me and we grinned at his foolishness.

"Seeing that I was pregnant, Peggy came over to us, delighted but concerned. Right in front of Matthew and the Reverend, she said, 'When you need me, Doris, you send Matthew to get me and I will be there, and I will bring the midwife.' The Reverend endorsed the idea, so that gave me great comfort.

"Ironically, that very night, after a bumpy ride home, I went into labour. Matthew rushed back to town to get Peggy. I knew something was wrong. All my other babies had gone full-term, but this one was small and had not moved inside of me for some time. With only my wee Brigitt to help me, I prepared the bed for the birth, like I had for the others.

"I don't remember Matthew returning with Peggy and Ina, the midwife. I was weak and barely conscious. The baby was passive, so Ina worked quickly, pulling the little body from my womb. It was a boy, she told me. I never saw him alive. 'Tiny thing, he was,' Ina said, 'very sad — not strong.'

"Ina, who only spoke a little English, saved my life! I don't know how she learned to do what she did — she didn't read — but she was the only midwife near town. She cleaned up everything and buried the little body out back amongst the birch trees.

"Matthew was completely disheartened, convinced he'd never have a son. He came in and cursed me. Screamed at me, 'Without a son, there will be no farm, no future! What use are you? I curse the day you came here!'

"Peggy and Ina had no sympathy for Matthew and pulled him outside. I could hear them arguing with him, telling him that I was weak and needed to rest. He yelled, 'I'm taking you back, get in the wagon!' But they refused. Then he tried to chase them away, screaming, 'Get the hell off my farm! This is my farm!'

"Eventually, he went off on his own. I was amazed that they were so brave, standing up for me against him. They were not going to leave me alone, with only five-year-old Brigitt to help me. They made a bed in the wagon and parked it close to the hut so they would hear me if I called out for help.

"We didn't sleep much. We found what was left of Matthew's bottle of rye and had a party. I had not talked openly with women since I'd left Ireland more than seven years ago now. We three were all so different, but at the same time connected by our time in the wild, trying to establish homes in the New World. It didn't matter where we women came from; we needed each other. We understood each other's circumstances.

"Ina had come to Canada with her sister when she was sixteen — it was all arranged in advance you see. They married brothers who didn't get along. Eventually she and her husband moved away from the family.

"Peggy told me that she and her husband had come from Liverpool on the same boat as Matthew and that he had been a good friend to them in the beginning. He was strong and skilled, full of plans for the future. He'd come into town, ill-kempt, but always with a gift of wild meat or berries. She would cook it up for the three of them while Matthew and the Reverend talked together in the parlour. That's where the idea of looking for a wife first started. He never invited them out to his place, but he described it to them in great detail. He told them about the spring-fed lake with clean water, which amused me. It was a slough that stank in the summer and made us all sick. We'd be covered in hives whenever we went in to bathe. I boiled the water, but it still smelt like urine, and was thick with slime that I filtered out with cheesecloth. Matthew kept promising me he'd dig us a well, but in the meantime I saved rainwater whenever I could.

"Over the years, Peggy saw him change. She assumed it was from being alone too much. They feared he would give up his efforts to farm. He needed a wife. Yes, she confessed, she had written the letters, and at one point understood that a young woman had agreed to come. That was me. She remembered that he came into town and bought a few new clothes before heading to Calgary. Months later, he told them that I didn't show up at the station as promised, and he was out a lot of money. They felt badly for him, knowing how hard he had worked. He said he'd given up with finding a wife.

"It was not until I ran away and the Reverend went to fetch him that they witnessed his bad temper. They were appalled by his behaviour. But the Reverend believed that it was his calling to keep marriages together. Promises made with God as a witness were to be kept, and he'd have nothing to do with ending our union. Peggy apologized for not being able to help me more, but I didn't blame her, of course.

"In the morning, Ina and Peggy made a big breakfast, and Matthew came in to eat. Before they left, Ina took him aside.

"I heard her say, 'No more babies. No more. Wife die.'

"He was infuriated that this Ukrainian woman would talk to him directly and told her to mind her own business. She argued that it was her business, that every woman was her business, and another shouting match erupted.

"Peggy was able to calm things down before leaving. She hugged me warmly and whispered, 'This can't go on. Take care of yourself and never doubt that things will get better.'

"Never had I felt so close and loved as I did by those two. At last I did not feel alone.

"But weeks went by and I didn't hear from Peggy. I got stronger and started to harvest the garden. Matthew worked on the house, rarely speaking to me.

"Brigitt was old enough to know that I was very unhappy and complained that she was, too. She didn't have any friends and she missed her sister. Sometimes she got moody and refused to help her father. He'd give her a whipping with his belt and she'd run away — hiding for days in the bush. When she did come home, Matthew was tough on her again and refused to feed her. He seemed bent on killing her, and I could see no end to this misery. As summer passed, I began to worry that she wouldn't survive the winter like this, staying out overnight. And she wouldn't survive his beatings.

"In late August she ran away and didn't come back. Matthew wouldn't let me go out looking for her and locked me up when he went to town. Unknown to me, she'd been watching the farm from a distance. When she saw her father leave in the wagon, she ran home and unbolted the door. The poor wee girl was in bad shape, thin and shaky; the soles of her feet were cracked and sore. She'd been eating saskatoons and vegetables from the garden when she managed to sneak back at night. I was attending to her, getting her cleaned up, feeding her, when, oh my Lord, I heard the wheels of a wagon approach. I hid her under the bed and went out to meet him.

"But it was Peggy. Her horse was lathered up and out of breath when she pulled into the yard. 'Come on, Doris, it's now or never!'

"'What are we doing?' I asked, amazed that she had appeared so unexpectedly.

"'We're getting you out of this hellhole! Where's Brigitt?'

"I grabbed what little I had and threw it into the wagon box. Within minutes, the three of us were heading west, Brigitt and I holding on for our lives, bouncing over the rough ground, too shocked to say much.

"Hours later, we arrived at a town called Rosedale. I could hear the train in the distance as we pulled up to the small station. Peggy explained that she had told several women of my situation and they had all contributed to the plan. When Matthew appeared at the General Store that morning, the wife of the store owner sent word to Peggy, and the women made their move. One woman got the wagon ready; another, the suitcases packed. Together they had gathered up what money they could. It wasn't much, but it would see me through a couple of months. My daughter, Maggie, would be on this same train, having caught it a half-hour earlier in their town, and it would take us all to Calgary.

"Peggy gave me a letter, with an address on the front, and told me that her sister was expecting us. She would help me find work sewing or cleaning or helping in some shop. As the train pulled in, I remember I hung onto Peggy — trying to gather my strength. She was so brave to have done this for me. She had taken such a risk.

"I was excited, yet afraid of the future. Having been subjugated for so long, I didn't know if I could manage the responsibility. If it wasn't for my girls, I would have done myself in long ago. But I hadn't and here we were.

"It was 1914. The train was full of farm boys on their way to Calgary where they could sign up to be soldiers. Like them, we were heading into the unknown, optimistic, hoping that the life ahead would be better than the one we were leaving behind.

"Matthew never knew what happened. Nor did any of the husbands in town — including the Reverend. It was a well-kept secret, and I'm sharing it with you."

She smiles, content with the ending. We sit in silence, and drink our tea.

Her story has stunned me. "I could never imagine such a life," I said. "My mother was born in 1910 on a homestead, not unlike the one you knew, out in the middle of nowhere. Her dad built a house that is still standing. The pictures of their lives are of the happy times, of course."

"I'm sure there are things they never told you," Doris responded. "It could not have been easy. Everyone suffered. The clothing alone was inadequate for the winters — leather boots, hand-knitted sweaters, and woollen coats. It was harsh, so harsh. How many children did your grandmother have?"

"Six. My mom was the eldest."

"Did they all survive?"

"Yes. My mom was fourteen when the last baby was born."

"Ah. Six in fourteen years." She nods knowingly to herself. "Could be she lost a few."

"Maybe."

Two women come into the room and start setting the tables. I realize our time is running short.

"But you, Doris, how did you make a living when you got to Calgary?"

"At first, I worked in a restaurant. In the kitchen. Hiding. Using another name. There were no laws to protect me. No possibility of divorce. No social assistance. I guess some things haven't changed all that much, from what I heard you say on the radio. I lived in constant fear of Matthew turning up. If he wanted me back, the police would have taken his side, without a doubt."

"But he didn't —"

"No, and I did pretty well. I made a life for my two girls and myself. With the war and so many men being away, more jobs were open to women. I learned how to type and eventually got work in an office."

"And Matthew? What became of him?"

She nods, as she decides how to sum it up. "Well. He didn't come looking for us, as far as I know. Maybe he thought we'd come back one day. Peggy told me that he secured the title of his land and worked on his house ... rarely coming into town. People were afraid of him, except for the Reverend who tried to reach out, but Matthew really became a hermit. When people did see him, he was bony and wild. He didn't take care of himself. He wasn't doing anyone any harm, so people let him be.

"Then one spring, Peggy wrote me — we always kept in touch through her sister — that Matthew had not shown up as usual in April to buy seeds and supplies. The Reverend and a couple of men rode out to the farm and found him dead.

His animals were on their last legs, penned in without feed. He was sitting in front of the huge stone fireplace he had built for his house — that's all he had managed to construct. It seemed clear to the men that he had lit the fire, a big fire, and had finished his bottle of rye before falling asleep and freezing to death.

"I felt guilty in a way. The man needed care, he needed help, but I was not willing to sacrifice the life of my girls — or my own, for that matter — so that he could survive."

"No one would ever blame you," is all I can think to say.

"Maybe his last dreams were good ones — dreams of living in his grand home, enjoying the fire. He didn't leave a will, so legally the farm belonged to the eldest son. There was no son, so it came to me. Maggie was already on her own, married, but Brigitt was still single and wanted to be a nurse. I came back, much to everyone's surprise, and sold the farm, then moved into Brooks — to be close to my one true friend. Peggy.

"When Peggy's husband died, a new pastor came in, of course. There was no place for her to go, so I invited her to come live with me. We had twelve wonderful years together. We were just like sisters, kind to each other, grateful to live on our own terms. Our house was the house that women came to if they needed a place to stay. And there were many. Most of them had children, so Peggy got her fill of children."

It seems time to ask the question I've come to ask: "Do you remember when women won the vote? Were you a part of that in any way?"

"Well, yes and no. That was 1916. I hadn't been in Calgary so very long. My girls were still young. But I did attend a couple of suffrage meetings ... and made a small donation."

"Did you meet any of them? Were they good speakers? Smart?"

"Well, I loved Mrs. McClung of course — she was Irish, you know, she had the gift of wit. I had read her books, over and over. But to be honest, I felt uncomfortable with some of the ladies who were, you know, city folk and a bit full of themselves.

"I was a poor woman, with a thick accent and no stature except that I appeared to be educated, in that I could read and write. The class system was very strong in those days, and I didn't fit in with those who had married well and were respected members of their community. They did not believe that all women should have a vote ... just the more acceptable ones."

"Really!" I am mildly shocked and disappointed.

"Yes, of course. It was quite different then. I know there were some who wanted the vote because they thought that women would make the country a better place to live. That Canada could be an example to the rest of the world. They had strong views about what 'better' meant. The Temperance Union was very motivated to prohibit alcohol, for instance — which did happen. Some righteous women thought that people who were mentally, you know, should be separated, put away ... even neutered. Oh yes!

"I identified with the farm women, who felt that they had not been supported by the government; that we needed support, we needed schools, community halls; that we'd been exploited — and we had."

"So you did think that winning the vote was a milestone, an important piece of history!"

"Yes, but it could have been more than it was. We could have been a powerful force, but so many women just voted

as they were told to vote, and when we did elect a woman —
Louise McKinney — she only held office for one term. Women
winning the vote did not change the world like we'd hoped.
They had not been educated to make a choice of their own.
Even today, lots of women don't make their own decisions."

Unfortunately, she is right.

"So, Doris," I feel she is getting tired now, and I should
sum up our talk. "You promised me that you would tell me
why prairie women were the first to get the provincial vote
in Canada."

"And I've done just that. I've told you!"

"You have? Then why?"

"Because it was evident that women were essential to the
settlement of this land. Farm women did at least half of the
work. They learned how to make everything from soaps to lax-
atives, raised a wide variety of animals and bred them. They
put in huge gardens, pickled and canned, dried and smoked
enough food to feed a family during the long, cold winter —
which could be eight months long!

"These women were superwomen who made living here
tolerable. There was no social structure out in the wilds.
No sports facilities. No shelters for the disadvantaged. No
welfare system. They organized the parties, the weddings, the
funerals, the social events. They took care of the sick and
the weary — and yet they remained nameless, as though they
didn't exist. They rarely heard their first names. They were
just 'Missus so and so' — somebody's wife.

"These women fought for schools, for hospitals. They
fought for the vote so that they would have a say. We had just
come out of a war, and women had proved themselves to be
more than capable in the absence of the men. They demanded

that right, the vote — and the powers that be could not deny their worth."

"Well said!" I almost applaud.

"Listen to me, speech-making. Peggy used to give the talks. She could tell you a thing or two. But now, she's gone. And I'm still here, in this oh-so-quiet place. So it's up to me. And I'm just about done. But I need you to promise me something."

She closes her diary. She has barely glanced at it.

"Of course!"

She pushes the diary toward me. "I'm giving you this ... it will help you, I hope. I tried to give it to the local museum — they did not want it. I wrote to the provincial and national archives. They didn't want it either. My family isn't interested. So I'm giving it to you."

"Are you sure?"

"Yes, I'm sure ... but I need you to promise —"

"Anything!"

"— that one day, somehow, you will tell my story, which is the untold story of so many who have gone without notice. Ours is a different kind of history, but it is just as real. My story is your story now, and if you don't do something with it, it will be lost. Do you understand that? Lost. And there are so many other stories to be uncovered — the best ones are often buried. Go to the graveyards — you will see. Young women buried with newborn babies. Whole families wiped out by a storm, or a prairie fire, or the flu of 1918. You will see men with two, three, four wives ... rarely women with two or three husbands. Promise me you'll not let us be forgotten."

"I promise."

I START OUT FOR HOME in the dark, but don't make it very far. The snow is whirling. My wipers soon get iced up and only clear narrow arcs of snow off my windshield. I can hardly see the road, which is covered in white, so I can only guess where the centre is by gauging the oncoming traffic. I wish I had seat belts that worked; this would be a time to put them on. Imagining a head-on collision, I pull over and get a room in a bleak motel just off the highway.

Doris Ward's story keeps plays over and over in my head.

In the morning, I head out. It's a glorious blue-sky day, with sunlight sparkling off the fresh layer of snow.

Instead of going straight home, I decide to take a long-delayed detour. I head east toward Edgerton — I have an urge to visit the grave of my grandmother and pay my respects to her and to the stories I can only imagine.

As I drive north, I notice the rusted gates and narrow roads that lead to the deserted homesteads that dot the vast farmland. Many old houses and barns have collapsed — the sad remains of hard work and dreams unfulfilled. I pull off the highway to take a picture of a single crabapple tree that remains out in the middle of an empty field. I imagine a woman with a big family, planting a large garden out there, and making crabapple jelly in the autumn — it was a lot of work without much thanks.

I always thought of my grandmother as being a little grouchy. I remember someone saying she was much too opinionated. She didn't tolerate misbehaviour, so I was always reserved when I was with her.

Most of our visits were anchored by a game of Rummy. We both loved the game and played it fast, without any talking.

She was smart — she always seemed to know what I had in my hand.

I never asked her anything personal of course; children were forbidden to ask questions. But when I was about ten, she surprised me with a private exchange. "Anne," she said, "don't get married until you are twenty-six and only have two children. You understand? It's important." I nodded, though it seemed like such an odd thing to say.

In retrospect, it was the best advice I ever received from an older woman. I avoided her when she was alive, but now I think we might have been friends.

Years later I would discover that she had grown up as a neighbour to Nellie McClung (née Mooney) had gone to school Nellie's younger siblings. The families stayed in touch and Nellie came down to the farm on occasion to visit Grandma. My mother wasn't fond of Nellie McClung, because after her visits, my grandparents would always have an argument. That made me laugh. I imagined that the infamous suffragette fuelled my Grandma's sense of justice. It pleased me even more, that Grandma named her first child, my mother, Nellie.

What would Grandma Carrie think of me now — age twenty-eight and childless, wishing I had known her better? Wishing I had asked her questions, and heard her stories. I know nothing of what she thought or lived. To the world she was Mrs. Donald Pawsey. To the family she was Mom or Grandma. I can't remember anyone using her first name.

Doris was right. The history of those with power will written down in a way that will favour them, but those who have lived and died outside the documented world are the ones that fascinate me now.

As word got out that we were interested in the personal untold stories of women who were homesteaders, we were overwhelmed by the response. By the time we finished the film, we had a room full of boxes stuffed with family photographs, personal letters, diaries, and unpublished works. We zigzagged across Canada doing interviews from Montréal to Victoria, and in 1975 the documentary film, *Great Grand Mother*, was finished by the National Film Board of Canada. The film is still available at **www. nfb.ca/film/great_grand_mother**. A year later a book, *A Harvest Yet to Reap*, was published, that featured a portion of the collection we had gathered. All these materials were eventually donated to the University of Saskatchewan.

BENEATH
IT ALL

Latitude 57, Fort McMurray, Alberta, 1973

FRESH WHITE SNOW shimmers in the moonlight as we enter the pristine forest on our snowmobiles. At nine in the morning, it is still dark this far north. Daylight lasts for only five hours here in January, so we want to set up before dawn breaks.

As shafts of light begin to define the day, we strap on our snowshoes and prepare our film equipment. It's a challenge to work here. With the snow several feet deep, nothing can be placed on the ground; it will sink out of sight.

This is a mixed boreal forest. Winters last up to eight months, and temperatures plummet to sixty degrees below zero. Life is harsh. Many creatures hibernate or fly south, but the real northerners, the permanent residents, are resilient and resourceful. They are likely watching us now, as we disturb their world with our noisy machines and human chatter. We are miles away from the mine, the work camp, or any other signs of "civilization." There are no power lines. No roads. No smoke rises in the distance.

It is going to be a bright day with a blue sky and no wind. Multiple animal tracks stamped in the fresh whiteness assure us that life is abundant here. Nature is well balanced after thousands of years of uninterrupted evolution.

We've brought two cameras, which we have wrapped up in electric blankets powered by a couple of car batteries. They would not run for more than a minute if they weren't protected. Today it's a mild thirty below, and the 16-mm film is brittle and could break with handling. We will have to reload a couple of times — it's finicky work and must be done with bare hands that quickly go numb. Our coats are bulky, our gloves big and clumsy. It's difficult to do the tasks that demand any precision, like focusing and using our light meters.

Our little film company, Filmwest, has secured a contract with Syncrude to make a documentary film about the Alberta tar sands. Specifically, we're looking at the ecological trade offs if the extraction proves to be financially viable and the mining becomes extensive. If the price of oil keeps rising the economic benefits will be obvious, but what about the environment? What will be sacrificed, and what can be reclaimed?

A smaller mine has been up and running for a number of years, harvesting this resource. Now Syncrude, a huge consortium, has entered the race, and they have hired a group of respected ecologists to assess the environmental problems and to come up with solutions. They have also hired us to record the efforts of these scientists — an indication of their openness and commitment to assume responsibility for the impact that a larger mine might have. We have embraced the project, as the research and results could have an enormous impact on our beloved Alberta.

We haven't decided who in Filmwest will direct this movie, but it is my turn, and with my science degree I'm vying for the opportunity. This pre-shoot is my opportunity to prove that I can keep up with "the boys" in these harsh conditions. But it is a challenge. The snowshoes could double for tennis rackets. With my short legs, I can only take tiny steps, with my feet spread far apart. Waddling about, I lack any sense of dignity or authority. Muscles, in unmentionable places, start aching the moment I strap the snowshoes on, but as the only woman on the team, I will grin and bear it. Having been a kid sister, with three older brothers, I know to keep all whining to myself. If I do end up directing this film, I'll have to endure much more than this.

Luckily, I've always felt at home in the wild. As a young woman I had an Appaloosa pony that I kept at my aunt's farm north of Edmonton. By the time I was twelve, my cousins and I would take off on Saturday mornings and wander at will on our horses, riding along the railway ditches, across endless fields, along the Sturgeon River, miles from the farm. Sometimes we'd stop and camp overnight — build a fire, heat up a can of beans, or roast some hot dogs we'd brought with us, and then sleep on our saddle blankets beneath the stars. No one worried about us, as long as we were home in time for supper at 6 p.m. on Sunday. Those days of freedom taught me a lot — I took a few falls, learned to care for my mare, got lost, and caught in bad weather, and learned how to find my way home. Mother Nature is a demanding but sensible teacher. I owe her a lot. Maybe this film will be my chance to pay back the lessons of my youth.

The mixed boreal forest of Canada is enormous. It covers an area ten times the size of California — but it is here, specifically in Northern Alberta, that the largest known reservoir of crude bitumen in the world lies hidden, just beneath the surface.

The Cree and the Chipewyan have known of its existence for thousands of years. It has revealed itself in various ways, oozing out of the ground or along the eroding Athabasca River bank. Sometimes it has caught fire — spawning legendary tales of the world below.

The object today is to get a variety of shots that reveal the life cycles that exist here, on this land, before it is cut open and mined. We work for hours without talking, knowing the wildlife is shy and wary. Cormorants, snow rabbits, deer, squirrels, and, in the distance, a wolverine are captured on film. We cheat a little and throw out some birdseed to attract some feathered friends; flocks of finches and chickadees flutter down to take our bait before being chased away by the ravens. It saddens me to think that we may be the last to see this little corner of the world as it is now, in its pristine form.

By early afternoon, I cannot ignore the fact that Nature is calling me. Though I have tried to refute the idea that my gender could in any way impede my ability to face the rigors of directing this film, my need is urgent. My bladder is full. What can I do? I can't even bend at the waist with all these clothes on, let alone squat. Being bottom heavy, I have never been able to squat, even on solid ground. If I do try to respond to Nature's call here, I am sure I will roll over bare-ass backwards, with my multiple layers of clothing rolled down around my ankles, feet spread wide to accommodate the snowshoes, and my head buried in the snow. Not a pretty sight.

Regrettably, but with as much dignity as I can muster, I announce that I am going to take one of the snowmobiles back to the work camp. They all know why. I'm glad I can't see their faces — I imagine they are smirking underneath their scarves. I could ask for help to execute my "mission," but I have decided that it's not an option. Damn! It's hard to admit that these three guys can do something I cannot.

"I'll get back as soon as I can," I declare, as if it is of great importance. "Just keep shooting without me." It is past noon and the sun will be gone by three. They just nod. The likelihood of my getting back in time to do much of anything is nil. I mount the snowmobile without grace, taking one mitten off with my teeth so I can get the thing started with one strong pull. Okay, so it takes three attempts before it revs into action.

Last year, the Alberta government, working with Syncrude, announced that they were investing a major amount of money into a special process that extracts oil from the tar sands. Developed originally in the 1920s, it works like this: Massive diggers scoop up raw bitumen from the open pit mine and load it onto gigantic trucks capable of carrying up to four hundred tons. They take it to an enormous processing plant, where it is dumped, then blasted with a mixture of hot water and detergent-like chemicals. The heavy sand in the bitumen separates from the oil and sinks. The oil remains in the froth that floats on top. It is skimmed off and sent on to another plant, probably in Edmonton, for further refinement. The hot contaminated water and sand are pumped into a retention pond, which is really a lake. This first mine will require one about ten by ten miles square — so big that it may change the route of migrating birds, and those that land on it will be in peril, coated with the sticky, oily waste. In the future, larger plants will create larger lakes.

We were amazed when the executives promised to give us full access to the land, the staff, and the plant itself. Since we started our research, they have made no effort to censor us. Nor have they censored their ecological team members, who speak openly about the possibilities. One major concern is that beneath the retention pond — there is porous muskeg that must be sealed in some way or the contaminated water will seep into the earth and eventually make its way to the Athabasca River system that flows into the Arctic Ocean.

I am about to pull out on my snowmobile when Kenny, the soundman, hops on the other sled and announces, "I'm coming with you. I brought the wrong microphone." I can't bear to wait for him. I know he will catch up to me, as my driving skills are questionable.

As the clouds roll in, the forest looks the same in every direction, so I'm happy to follow the packed path we made when coming in this morning. In the summer, many streams and small lakes define this region. For more than ten thousand years, the Indigenous peoples have sustained themselves here by fishing, gathering, trapping, and hunting. Now they are fearful that the mine will poison the environment and threaten all life that draws water from the Athabasca Basin.

Syncrude and the other oil companies have promised that the mines will bring prosperity to the region. In partnership with the government, they are offering a variety of training and business opportunities that will give the Indigenous population access to exclusive financial assistance. Tens of thousands of people will be employed, operating the machinery and maintaining the plant. Schools, a college, and a hospital will bring in professionals; retail will be profitable, serving a population that is making good money. Already, Fort

McMurray is booming with people moving here from around the world, anxious to cash in. The population has more than doubled in the past ten years to about seven thousand people. That will double again in the next couple of years — yesterday's newspaper said that five thousand new jobs were up for grabs right now. The pressure to go full throttle is intense. Huge money is at stake, and the government is betting heavily that the future will be financed with the "black gold" that lies just beneath the surface.

Like everyone else, I am guilty of benefiting from this huge exploitation. I have written dozens of proposals, trying to get another personal film financed, but it's difficult, especially when most of my subjects have to do with women. If I get to direct this film, it will legitimize my career; I will make more than I would ever have made as a schoolteacher. I could afford to devote more time to getting my own projects off the ground.

Syncrude is giving us an ample budget and is showing respect, taking us seriously, it would seem. I hope we are a part of the solution and not just a piece of the propaganda used to reassure people that this will bring a better future. We are not totally naïve — we know that this film could make them look good, especially if there are some scientific breakthroughs.

I struggle to push down my doubts, as the snowmobile trail brings me to a large lake we circled earlier. Feeling desperate to relieve myself, I decide to cut across the frozen water. It is a faster and more direct route to the work camp — and to the toilet.

I look back and see Kenny catching up behind me. Waving and pointing to the lake, I convey my decision, and he waves back in agreement. I roar over the bumpy shoreline and slide onto the icy surface. There are places where the wind has swept the ice clean so that it mirrors the sky, giving me a sense that I can fly.

I can't hear a thing over the scream of my snowmobile. With the throttle wide open, and the wind blasting against my face, I delight in zigzagging and having a bit of fun as I traverse the glassy expanse. This is so much easier than plowing through deep snow! I stand up, and whoop like the barrel racer I once was — this is fantastic!

Suddenly the pitch of my engine shifts and I am snapped out of my glee. My speed decreases as the roar turns into a low-end whine. Totally confused, I feel the engine choking as I begin to sink into sludge. The ice beneath me gives way and I come to a full stop. The water creeps up onto the ice, freezing as soon as it hits the air.

I stand up on the saddle of my mechanical beast and yell to Kenny to "Turn back!" and "Stay clear!" before he gets bogged down like me! He can't hear me, of course, but figures out that something is wrong and slows down. Registering the danger, he makes a sharp turn away and stops just in time to see my snowmobile — and me — disappear in one terrifying gulp, dropping into the frigid water.

I have so many clothes on that, at first, I only feel a burning sensation licking at my neck and wrists, where the icy water quickly finds its way to my skin. With my thick-mitted hands, I paw away at the edge of the hole I have created, trying to get some kind of grip, but the frozen perimeter keeps breaking away. I can't find a place where I can pull myself out. There is no rigid shelf between the water and the surface. It's just mush.

I can see that Kenny is off his snowmobile, testing the solidity of the surface around him, trying to decide what to do. How close can he get to me on foot without risking his own life?

The cold water is seeping in through the zippers and seams of my clothing now. My boots are slowly filling with water and getting heavy. I can't decide whether I should kick them off or not.

At this temperature, water freezes in an instant. My mittens are solid blocks of ice. They have no flex; I cannot grab anything. I am in the middle of a lake, far from branches, ropes, or anything else that could be used to haul me out of this frigid opening, which grows wider and wider with my attempts to climb out.

I am flailing now, slowing down, growing stiff, unable to bend — but my mind is racing. What's happening? Why is the lake not frozen? It's too bizarre! Am I going to die out here — all because I couldn't pee in the winter woods? My gawd! This would be a crazy way to go.

Kenny tries to get closer, but retreats when he hears the ice cracking.

I have an idea and yell out, "Towmiyomicrofooo!" My mouth is quivering, barely functioning. He can hardly hear me with his head wrapped in a scarf, toque, and fur-edged hood.

"Mike-crow-phone!" I try again, exaggerating as much as I can. He gets it!

Racing back to his machine, he pulls out his microphone, long cord and all. Swinging it above his head, like a cowboy roping a calf, he lets out a little more length with each rotation. Placing his aim, he hurls it toward me — but it lands outside my reach. The situation is becoming dire; I'm getting heavier and heavier, weaker and weaker.

With Kenny pulling it back, the microphone bounces on the ice.

Again, he spins it around and around until its trajectory is consistent. Then, he lets it go.

This time it plops down right beside me in the slush. I can't bend my arms, but I am able to wind the cord around my wrist. Beyond that, I'm not much help. I have lost communication with my muscles; nothing works anymore.

Dry and naked, I weigh about 130 pounds, but now I'm a dead weight, shrouded in at least 50 pounds of soaking, wet clothing. Getting me out and onto the surface is difficult. Kenny tries from every direction, circling the watery hole, but I keep getting bogged down in the mushy ice. Finally, he finds an angle that provides a natural exit, so he is able to drag me up and over the lip of the crust and onto the ice. My wet clothes freeze immediately and I am encapsulated in a frozen cocoon — my right arm is rigid, stretched above my head, still connected to the cord, making me six feet long.

I hear him muttering as he drags me away, far from the hole, making sure we are on solid ice. Grabbing my hood, he gets me to his snowmobile. He cannot bend me to sit me down, so he attempts to balance me across the back of his seat, perpendicular. Swinging his leg high up above me, he manages to get on and start the motor, but as soon as he moves forward, I shift and roll off the back.

We start over and he tries to hold onto me, but again I slide from his grasp and land face down. He's getting tired.

I find myself watching his efforts from above — detached from the real danger. What I see is funny and I start to laugh.

It's like I am watching myself perform in a skit from a television show from my childhood — I'm Carol Burnett or Lucille Ball and I'm in a brilliant comedy routine. What a perfect epitaph, I think to myself — "She died laughing!"

There is no pain, just a warm fuzzy numbness and a hazy sense of the surreal. I'm encased in ice and Kenny can't get a good grip, so we cross the lake in this piecemeal manner, a few yards at a time, until we reach the shore.

Now we face the narrow winding path we made when snowmobiling through the forest this morning. Riding with me balanced perpendicularly across the seat is not an option. The trees on either side will wipe me off immediately.

The ice around my eyes makes everything blurry. Kenny bends down to see if I'm still alive, and I see his fuzzy form shadowing the light. Exhausted, he is breathing heavily as he gets right down within inches of my face. "Can you hear me?" I burble back from my other world. He nods. "I can't hear anything with all this stuff on! I'm going to have to drag you … don't know what else to do."

In championship time, he wraps the sound cord around my ankles, cinching it with a knot. Then, hanging onto the microphone, he gets back in his saddle and begins to pull me, feet first, behind him.

I am not completely sure what's happening now. Looking up at the sky as we weave through the trees, I see a psychedelic symphony of light and distortion. And even though the snowmobile is roaring with exertion, for me it is absolutely silent, as though someone has turned off the sound. My rigid torso slides along the narrow path like a sled.

I'm still aware, though I have no sense of my body. My mind is racing, still asking questions. Is the joke really on us?

Why is the water in this lake unfrozen beneath the surface? Is hot water from the retention pond making its way through the muskeg already? Even in the dead of winter — at this temperature?

With minimal resistance, we pick up speed. It's all so trippy with the sun strobing through the trees, creating flashes of rainbows and cosmic explosions. There is nothing I can do, so I surrender completely, and feel at peace with my eyes partially glued open and life suspended.

When we get to the trailer camp, they carry me into the medical centre. A small hole is still open in my "casket," and I can feel the burble of breath constantly reaching for life. I hear a cushion of whispered voices. There seems to be a lot of excitement and concern. I am weightless, but still moving — it is as though I am being called back from a sanctuary deep inside myself.

They crack open the ice around my face, and my head is liberated. They talk to me, but I can't respond. I can't understand them. What I hear is babbling nonsense. Random words jump out at me: "eyes — oxygen — lake — fingers — toes — miracle —"

The face of an older man, a calm soul, pops into semifocus, smiling at me, reassuring me that I will be fine. He looks like my father, like a god, and I believe him.

As they get rid of my icy shell, I go in and out of consciousness.

I flash back to the moment of revelation, when I realized that the ice wasn't frozen, that the snowmobile was sinking. The epiphany plays and replays in my mind, a recurring nightmare — I have a sick feeling of betrayal, disappointment. What is happening forms a hodgepodge in my brain, stuttering in its attempt to understand: Why wasn't the lake frozen out there?

A message from beneath is trying to reach me: the warm water of the lake must be Nature's way of telling me that all is not as it seems.

Once they break open my parka, I feel released. Now I can breathe more deeply and my head starts to clear. How many men are in this trailer, all staring at me, working on me? Someone is pulling off my boots; someone else is cutting off my ski pants. They are trying to save my life, working quickly, but I am horrified, embarrassed. I try to speak.

"Stop!" I try to say with as much strength and assertiveness as I can muster — but it comes out as a squeak, indecipherable. The older man comes back into view and looks concerned. "We need to get your clothes off. We need to get you warm. Your body temperature is very low."

"No," I plead, "I can do it myself."

That slightly amuses him. "We'll keep you covered ... no one will see you ... would that help, yes?" He nods at his team and they grab some extra blankets but —

"No! Please stop!"

I can see Kenny watching from the doorway, looking worried. "She was in the water for a long time...in fact, she was hysterical, laughing like a madwoman."

The gentle man addresses the room, "Everyone but Peter (a young medic) get out of here — I will call you back in when I need you ..."

I can feel myself shaking now. Maybe Kenny is right; I am not myself yet. Consciousness of my body is just beginning to return, and I'm in shock.

The man covers me with a big warm blanket and works quickly. "All right now. We have to get these wet things off." He sounds strict, like we're running out of time. I'm a child and he's a parent, taking care of me. But still I am reluctant — I want to stop him —

"Please ... don't." I have to take him into my confidence. "I ... I ..."

"You what? Is something hurting, something broken?"

"No ... back there, when I was laughing ... I ... peed myself ... and ..."

He starts to laugh. "You peed yourself! Really?" I am momentarily put off by his laugh. But he continues, "Well, that's it then! My God!"

That's what? I wonder. My nervous system is reconnecting and my mind is whirling.

He shakes his head in disbelief, "That explains it! I wondered how you managed to survive. The urine raised the temperature inside your icy shell and kept you from freezing to death. Thank the gods for your sense of humour, young woman ... your laughing, your peeing, saved your life!"

Like magic, my pants are instantly removed, and I am rolled into a warm blanket and wrapped up tightly like a newborn baby.

The room starts to spin again like I've had too much brandy. Drunk on life, I start to laugh again at what I remember of Kenny and me trying to cross the lake. I remember my howling with hilarity, the cloud of humidity rising like a smoke signal from the open hole in the ice. Where did that warm water come from? That's what I want to know.

A few days later, after babying myself over the weekend at home, indulging in hot baths and hard liquor, I climb the stairs to our offices in Edmonton, to see the rushes from the forest and to talk about how to move the project forward. I suppose we'll decide who will direct the film today.

When I arrive, the images are already flickering on the screen, and the guys are watching them silently. They like what they are seeing.

I am gearing myself up to talk about my suspicions — that there is something we are not being told. My concerns are just instinctual, not factual. Is this film is just a ruse, a distraction, a false assurance that the mining company and the government care about the impact on what they have described as "scrap land": You can't farm it; the timber isn't worth much. I take a seat and watch the remaining footage — how am I going to put these thoughts into words?

The screening ends and we all grab a coffee before starting our meeting. No one mentions my "accident." It's as though nothing out of the ordinary happened — it was just another crazy near miss and we've had lots of those: I went for a cold swim and lost a snowmobile, but I survived. That's yesterday's news.

Obviously Syncrude didn't make a big deal out of losing the snowmobile or I would have heard about it — I guess one Ski-Doo isn't even a speck on their balance sheet. Unless they are pushed, they won't look into why the ice on the lake had melted. Is there any point? That land is doomed regardless. No one wants to jump in front of this tidal wave of commerce that is going to hit the economy, resulting in the biggest mine ever imagined in North America.

But then, what if the Athabasca River becomes polluted and eventually runs into the Arctic Ocean and —

"So," says Dale, with his usual wide and wonderful smile, "are you ready to direct this movie, Wheeler?"

I am shocked out of my reverie. Stunned. I thought I'd have to fight for the position. But here they are, just handing it to me. "It's your turn." They all agree without question.

What do I do? My concerns remain, but I immediately start to justify taking the job. Maybe I can address my concerns as we move forward. I will press the scientists to be truthful and public. Ask the hard questions. If we don't grab this opportunity, we will not be there to see for ourselves what is happening. Maybe we are pawns, working for big business, but this extraction is going to happen regardless, and little me is not going to stop it. At the very least, I can bear witness and we can share what we know — hopefully that will make a difference.

It is amazing how quickly I can turn myself around. Without raising my hand, without expressing my concerns, without questioning my own motives, I accept the position of director with a voice full of excitement and drive. "It's going to be a great film, an important film! Thank you, guys, for supporting me on this!" I hear myself say.

But my inner voice — the one that spoke to me that day on the lake — will come back to remind me for the rest of my life that some questions were never asked and some problems have never been solved. I will think of the hole in the ice — in the middle of that pretty little lake — every time I see pictures of the massive open pit that is the mine, or read about the high rates of cancer in Fort Chipewyan possibly due to water contamination, or hear accounts about the mutated fish caught in the Athabasca River hundreds of kilometres north of Fort McMurray. By 2017 the mining efforts covered an area of 220 square kilometres.

BY THE END OF THE YEAR, the little lake and the forest around it will no longer exist. That whole area will lie beneath the big retention "pond." Time will tell what can or cannot be reclaimed. Civilizations are built on trade offs and I have accepted a few of my own.

We finished the documentary and in the end called it *Trade Offs*. I was proud of the film, of the work done by all of us, of the scientists who spoke openly, of the animation that clearly depicted the process used to extract the oil from the tar sands, now referred to as oil sands — so that people could ask their own questions. We were confident that the movie would be shown widely. It was politically balanced — giving voice to both sides of the environmental debate. But sadly, for me and for Filmwest, the materials, including the original footage, sound tracks, animation cells, A and B rolls, test prints — everything needed to make prints for distribution — were confiscated by Syncrude. They paid for it, owned it, and decided to pull the plug. *Trade Offs* was never screened publicly.

I'll never really know what lay beneath that decision, but for me it was a turning point. I had gone against my better instincts, being ambitious, rationalizing that it would further my career.

I needed to rethink my choices. It isn't enough to make a good film. Film, I realized, is an art, yes. But it is also a tool — and it is what is done with that tool, that matters.

THE DEVIL
AND THE DIVINE

Bombay, India, 1976

HERE I AM, fresh off the plane from Edmonton, sitting on a curb in Bombay, waiting for a cab to take me to an ashram six hours south of here. Alone in a foreign land, I'm keeping to myself, fortified by my army surplus uniform, complete with thick-soled boots. I'm a no bullshit, strong-armed, liberated, keep your hands offa me kind of gal.

An elegant, older Indian woman sits down beside me. She is staring at me, studying my clothes before looking at me straight in the eyes. It's a look that feels familiar, a look of knowing. It's as though she understands what I am thinking. What does she see? That my being here is a mistake? That I am running away from something? I look away, trying to ignore her.

"Excuse me please." She demands my attention, then cocks her head and shimmies her shoulders. "Why are you dressed like a man?"

It is not her business. I shrug and turn away. I'm in a foul mood, too tired to get up and move away from her. Besides, there's nowhere else to sit. I'll just concentrate on writing my postcard. She'll get the message.

With a snap of her fingers, two cups of chai on a tray magically appear and she offers me one. Using my lower voice of power, I respond, flatly, "No thanks."

I assume she's all about the money. She wants to sell me something, hoodwink me, trick me. I'm blonde, buxom, and blue-eyed — an obvious target.

"Please, try it! It's chai, tea. Very good."

She holds the tea close to me. "It will refresh you. You look so hot and tired. Please. I see you are from somewhere else."

What the hell? Why me? There are lots of other Westerners wandering about, much much richer than me.

She remains gracious and looks concerned. Her lilting accent sweetens her advance. "I cannot drink two cups of tea. Please, take it." Her expression is so alluring and she's not going away. It does smell good.

"You are very kind. But no, thank you."

She continues to scan every inch of my body with her gaze. I've been travelling now for more than forty-eight hours, without sleep, and am feeling dizzy from exhaustion and heat. I must look and smell disgusting. My hair is greasy and flat and I would die for a bath. I shift away from her.

"Look at your boots! Are you in the military?" I look at her closely for the first time. She is wearing a beautiful sari and dainty sandals. A lovely ribbon that glows in the sunlight holds back her long thick hair. Her jewellery sparkles in the sun, even though it's made of plastic. She wears bangles on her arms and legs and a dainty nose ring. Centred above her huge, inquiring eyes is a dazzling red bindi that flashes at me, again and again. I am dazzled.

"Well? Are you? A soldier?"

"No," I reply, keeping it short.

"But these are heavy wool pants ... and this shirt, a man's shirt, yes?"

"I do a lot of physical work and these clothes are practical for what I do."

She considers that for a moment. "You are not working now."

"No," I admit, "I'm not."

"You are a lovely young woman and you want to be a man!"

The words spew out of me. "No! I don't! I don't want to be a man! Because I am not a man!" My own reaction surprises me. She has certainly pushed a psychological button. She's either very perceptive or she's reading my mind.

I recently resigned from a film collective that has been at the centre of my life for the last six years. My membership ended in a moment of rage, which I regret, but as the only woman filmmaker, I felt I was on the outside of an argument, again, trying to prove myself worthy of equal membership. Perhaps I was oversensitive, but my accumulated frustrations had reached a peak during a meeting over job assignments, and I exploded.

Real or perceived, I felt as though Filmwest — the company, or collective, as we sometimes called it — was fractured, and the egalitarian "model" we had established was falling apart. We didn't all have equal power, equal say, or equal talent for certain roles assigned. Some of us did more work than others, but we all got paid the same. I completely lost my temper over something trivial and left in such turmoil that I fell down the back stairs of our office and broke my leg.

Honestly, it had been a long time coming. We'd been together through thick and thin and we had learned a lot.

I was the first to leave and am feeling physically and emotionally exhausted.

My broken leg necessitated me staying put for some time, which was good. I had to give my situation some thought. I decided to get away for a while. It was time to travel on — and India was at the top of my "places to go" list.

So, here I sit, on a curb in India, wondering what am I going to do now? I'm not sure I want to make films on my own. It's hard enough to put together a movie with the support of a group. Starting over again from scratch, alone, seems daunting. Maybe I will have to find something else to do with my life.

The woman is still looking at me. "There are so many good things about being a man, don't you think? They have so many advantages."

She *has* been reading my mind. "Excuse me?" I say in disbelief.

"Men have so many advantages, yes? Those who don't see that are delusional. It's not really a level playing field, is it?"

Her question has jolted me. "No, it sure isn't. But it should be." I didn't expect to be having a gender equality discussion sitting on the lip of a gutter, across from the Dakar taxi station, but here I am.

She smiles and nods. "Yes. It would be a better world if the feminine and the masculine were better balanced. I think, long ago, it might have been so — but today, the world has become unnatural, tipped. What women do is not valued."

I nod. I accept the tea that she is still offering. I take a sip. It is delicious and I hum with pleasure.

She is pleased that I like it. "Very good. And you came from where, please?"

"Canada. Western Canada."

"And all women dress like that there?"

I am amused. "Not quite like this, no. But it is winter there now, so when I left ... I wore this to the airport."

"I see! Of course. You have other clothes in your bag? Yes? Dresses?"

"I have a dress. Yes."

"Only one dress?"

"Yes, one," I confess, "and some pants and shorts...."

Shaking her head sadly, she gets up. "You are a confused young woman. You have no idea where you are. Please, come with me."

"Where? No, I can't. Sorry. I'm waiting for the taxi to Pune."

"The taxi comes every hour on the hour. You can catch the next one. This will not take long. Believe me, you will expire in that outfit — it is totally wrong. You have come to India, so be in India!"

I promised myself when I left Canada that I would do what I wanted, when I wanted, how I wanted. I would choose my own course, with no need to find consensus, open to anything. Shockingly, having just landed, this encounter seems predestined. She's like a fairy godmother, appearing from nowhere, sensing my needs.

The truth is, I don't have to be anywhere, today or tomorrow. No one knows I'm coming. No one is expecting me anytime soon. I told my friends in Pune, I would come in February, or March, or maybe never. I could accept this woman's offer, take this detour, and no one would care. For some reason I completely trust her — she is delightful and very enticing. On impulse, I grab my bag, "Okay, let's go!"

She pulls me across the busy street, intricately choosing our way through bikes, cars, motorcycles, cows, camels, trucks, and rickshaws that are brushing past us — moving at different speeds, in every direction, some crossing over and between us. Her timing is perfect. There can be no hesitation, no indecision in this rush of traffic. Either you are totally aware and synchronized, or you are wiped out. The most important rule soon becomes clear — "The bigger you are, the more rights you have." It's always the little one's fault.

We leave the lively road and enter a narrow alley, choked with humanity. I stay close to her as we snake through the crush of people, some setting up their stalls, others performing their daily bathing and grooming. I call out to her over the din, "What's your name?"

"Jyoti. And yours?"

I think my name is too short in most languages, so I automatically tell her, "Anna."

Completely turned around and lost, I dare not lose sight of her, as I try to take it all in. I'd never find my way back.

The air is thick with the stench of stale cooking oil, burning dung, rotting vegetables, urine, and body odour. These people have no privacy. They are the street dwellers — some young and beautiful, some ancient, some close to death. We duck under cloth awnings, dull with age and bird droppings, and cross through a laneway, lined with men sitting on the ground with fabric all around them, sewing with their hand-cranked machines. Some of them stop what they are doing and stare at me with interest. Women, crouched in corners, cook over open fires, and others feed their babies; a lone cow drinks soapy water from a drain that flows from what must be a laundry. Fascinated, I stop to look around, but am immediately pulled away by Jyoti, who has looped back to get me.

She pulls me through a back gate under the low archway of a three-storey building and enters a small, quiet courtyard.

"Here you can have a shower," Jyoti announces.

Tucked in a corner, behind a single wall, is a pipe sticking out of the cement. Over the end hangs a tin can with holes punched into its bottom, effectively creating a shower.

Jyoti pulls a curtain across the open side. "Nobody will disturb you. Get refreshed, I will take care of everything." She hands me a bar of soap and a thin cotton towel.

Grinning, she takes my backpack. "Don't worry, I won't steal your blue jeans!" With that, she disappears.

What about my passport? I momentarily panic.

Oh well. I have surrendered to her plan. Why? I don't know. She's gone and I'm keen to get clean. I peel off my sticky clothes. Looking up, I realize that hundreds of people live here. Above me I see stairways, doorways, and open corridors. I quickly duck out of sight.

The water is cool and the soap is scented with sandalwood. I feel so good, I start to sing, a bit giddy with jubilation.

"I'm gonna lay down my heavy load, down by the river-side, down by the riverside, down by the riverside...." I hear a titter from above and look up. Two toddlers lean over a railing, looking down at me, unblinking. Such eyes they have. I wave. They wave back.

By the time I finish my shower, a pair of beaded sandals and a robe have replaced my clothes and boots. I get dressed and Jyoti reappears, holding my one dress.

"This is too short. You cannot wear that here, no, no, no. You come with me."

I follow her down a hallway to a small room, a dressing room, with several short-sleeved sari tops hanging on one wall.

"Please, put on the blue blouse and yellow slip for now." She closes the door for privacy.

I struggle to fit into the tiny top. There has been a mistake. I call out to whoever may be there, "Excuse me. I think the blouse is about ten sizes too small!"

"Let me see!" Jyoti whips open the door and takes a look. "No, no, no, that is very good!"

My bosoms are squashed up so high that they brush against my chin when I look down. This can't be right. The seams are so stretched that each stitch looks like it is about to pop.

But Jyoti is pleased, "I love the colour. Perfect."

Two young women squeeze into the tiny room and wordlessly begin to spin me around, folding and tucking and wrapping me in cloth.

"No, really no ... I can't wear this...." It's so ridiculous, I start to giggle. They are delighted with my full figure and ample bosom. The shiny silk cloth is wildly colourful, tie-dyed with arcs of overlapping colours like the tail feathers of a peacock — teal, purple, yellow, pink, and gold!

Completely draped, I am shuffled out into the hall. "This is much too bright for me!"

"Not to worry!" says Jyoti. "We have many, many ... you can try more!"

"I cannot afford this ... I'm not rich."

"It is not so expensive. Come see."

Leading me down a hallway, they open a big door to the main room. It is a huge sari shop with its front windows facing a wide, busy street. The walls, at least fifteen feet high, are stacked to the top with magnificent and extravagant fabrics. Customers sit on large cushions as bolts of cloth are pulled from the shelves and unravelled, cascading before them with shimmering finesse. I see a dazzling display of silks and satins, cottons and linens, hand-sewn with sequins and other fine stitchery, all of it breathtaking.

"You can see the finest saris here. Some have taken years to complete," explains Jyoti. "Very expensive — but yours, not so much."

Thrilled, she ushers me toward a well-lit, full-length mirror. "See what a beautiful woman we have with us today!"

The whole room turns. "Ah!" they exclaim.

This woman, me, moves into the picture that is the mirror. Bangles and earrings, toe rings and ankle bracelets appear from nowhere and are placed upon me, as I stare at myself, framed in such glory. I have never considered myself pretty — I was the tomboy and a bit chubby.

Inexplicably, tears well up in my eyes. I cannot speak. The unearthly being before me must be some kind of illusion. I don't know her. She is stunning, sexy, and shimmering with life.

I take a few steps closer, amazed — and trip on my own hem. Immediately, six yards of silk, the whole sari, collapse onto the floor. The women squeal with surprise. Thankfully, the simple slip keeps me modest.

"You can't walk like that, in big steps!" Jyoti laughs, "You must walk with grace — smoothly — not like a truck driver." She imitates me — "Boom, boom, boom, boom!" Everyone laughs, as the young women put me back together again in a jiffy.

It's true — my steps are heavy, long, and flat-footed. My legs are short. For most of my life I have been trying to keep up with "the guys." I often scurry, sometimes breaking into a run.

My three older brothers didn't wait up for me — I learned not to expect any favours from them. They accused me of being spoiled because I was the youngest and a girl. Maybe I was.

Working in film, I have had to prove that I can carry as much as any man. I swear my arms are longer by several inches after five years of hauling equipment and my legs are even shorter than they were.

This time, the dressers secure the sari at my waist with a large safety pin. "Let's see you now, Anna," says Jyoti. "Move like a woman carrying a sleeping child." She demonstrates, and I follow her slowly around the room, becoming increasingly less awkward and wooden. The fabric brushes back and forth against my legs, swinging with each footstep, and eventually I find a gentle rhythm. It's a decidedly sensuous experience, and I like it.

"How many rupees is it?" I venture.

"I will trade you for a pair of blue jeans," Jyoti quickly replies. I laugh.

"That seems more than fair," I agree.

February 11, 1976
Dear Mom,
Mailing this from Bombay en route to Pune. Going to visit Maureen McFarland for a few days. You remember her? You know her mother, Nancy. Maureen is living in Pune. I will stay with her for a few days before heading to Goa, then go by boat to Karachi and, hopefully, find your old house. Everyone is very polite here, just as you described. The people are beautiful, especially the young women with their thick dark hair and glorious decorated eyes.
Your loving daughter, Anne

WITH THE SARI VEILING MY FACE and body, I blend into the textures of India. Nobody notices me in the back seat of the taxi, ploughing its way out of the city, heading south. The driver keeps looking in his rear-view mirror, perplexed by me. I am an anomaly, I suppose, dressed up like this and all alone. I stare out the window, watching snippets of India flicker by like scenes from a disjointed movie. Beautiful Bollywood movie stars smile down on me from giant billboards, like gods. Children run in packs, scrounging in ditches — dangerously close to the trains that rattle past, churning up clouds of dust and smoke.

It's so intense and shocking that I cannot fully digest what I see. The heat, the smells, the colours, and the noise — life goes on like this all day, every day, forever.... I'm grateful for this privileged ride, shielded by a window from this overwhelming explosion of humanity.

And I am exhausted.

Eventually, the road widens into a two-lane highway and we pick up speed. An old Bentley, black and immaculate, passes us silently, carrying a load of tropical birds on its roof. Pedestrians give way to bikes, bikes to scooters, scooters to cars, cars to trucks, trucks to buses — and everyone gives way to the cows. The driver swerves left and right, zigzagging through the continuous maze of movement. With one near miss after another, I have no choice but to put my life in his hands.

As we break into the countryside, the stench of diesel fuel and human excrement diminishes, and I take a deep breath. The driver, an older man, rolls down his window. "Would you like some music?" he asks, respectfully.

"That would be lovely," I hear myself say, sweetly. Where did that princess voice come from? My little sandals dangle from my toes. I am done up like a Christmas candy in this fancy wrapping, feeling far too delicious and downright vulnerable. I cover my bosoms with my long scarf and avoid his gaze. If I had to run, I would not get very far. Nor would I be able to defend myself.

The cowgirl within me raises her voice, "What in hell are you thinking, girl? Here you are again. Nobody in the world knows where you are and yet you decide to doll yourself up, with your boobies popping out of your blouse, as you head into the night with a driver you don't know, to a place that you couldn't find on the map. You are as dumb as an ox!"

On the other hand, I like the disguise. We pass through small towns and stop to get gas. Even with my blonde hair and pale blue eyes, I am hidden in the shadows, and go unnoticed. No one comes up to my window begging, holding up a half-dead baby, like a woman did at the airport. In a way, I'm invisible.

"Sure, you are," says my inner cowgirl, "like a tropical bird, ready to be plucked."

I find my Swiss Army knife in my sack and, for lack of a pocket, shove it down my cleavage. It diminishes the rush of anxiety that has been messing with my sense of adventure.

The Indian music coming out of the speakers behind my head slides seamlessly up and down, high and low, like a swing, lulling me to sleep. I can't help it. I've been awake for almost two days and my battery is dead. Against my better instincts, I drift off into a deep sleep.

"EXCUSE ME, MEMSAHIB?" The driver has pulled over to the side of the road. "We are in Pune now. Where are you going exactly? Do you have an address?"

Groggy, I burrow into my backpack and pull out a letter

from Maureen with an address beneath the logo of the ashram. "Seventeen Koregan Park," I read. Taking the letter from me, he holds it under the light from the street and reads the whole thing.

"Rajneesh!?" he exclaims. "You are going to see this Rajneesh man?"

"You've heard of him?"

The driver shakes his head in disbelief. "This man? They call him the sex guru. He used to give talks in the park — close to where I kept my taxi in Bombay. When he came, the whole area would turn into a zoo! Full of hippies having sex everywhere. Like wild animals!"

"No!" I laugh, unbelieving.

He turns around in his seat and grabs me with his look, so serious. He sees no humour in my response. "They all wear orange," he says, scowling. "We call them 'the orange people.' Some live like sadhus, nearly naked. I am glad you are wearing blue. Blue is good."

"Well," I try to calm him, "I am visiting an old friend from university. You don't need to worry about me."

He is not convinced. "Do not go near this man. He will steal your mind, make you do things you do not want to do, make you wear orange."

I can't help but be amused and shake my head, dismissing his warning.

He barks at me now, grabbing my arm. "Don't trust him. We got rid of him — ran him out of Bombay. He's a dangerous man."

"He's not dangerous. Radical perhaps but —"

He cuts me off. "Do you believe in free love?"

I don't like the look in his eyes; he has lost his gracious

fatherly charm. He grips my arm tightly. I try to pull away, getting angry.

"Well," I venture, "I think love should be free, people should be free to love whomever they wish.... I don't think a woman, for instance, should need a dowry." I have crossed a line now, by speaking my mind. I am not the helpless young woman he needs to protect.

I could not stop myself from mentioning the dowry — the tradition of a bride's family having to give a groom's family a substantial amount of money or gold or property (which is sometimes more than they can afford), to ensure that the marriage will happen. A family with many daughters can be cursed by this burden. The value of the dowry, especially in an arranged marriage, can determine what kind of life the woman will have within her new family. I think it is insulting to all women to be measured in this way.

He is infuriated by my audacity and turns off his car. His voice goes cold and gruff. "This is the central taxi stand. Please pay me the fare. With tip."

"But I gave you the address —"

"Get out of my taxi please! You can take a rickshaw from here."

Feeling strongly chastised and discombobulated, I pay, gather up my things, and leave without a backward glance.

As soon as I shut the door, a three-wheeled motor rickshaw pulls up beside me. The young, snappy driver hops out, grabs my backpack, and tosses it into his tuk-tuk. This is good because my sari has shifted, and I feel like I must hold it together with both hands as I climb into his back seat.

"My name is Veda," he says with a friendly smile. "You are going to ashram, yes?"

"Yes, please!" I answer, relieved.

His little scooter is decorated with images of Hindu gods, prayer flags, and blinking lights. I hang on as we make a quick u-turn and join a stream of rickshaws, all of them stuffed with "orange people," heading toward Koregan Park.

He turns up his sizeable stereo and I hear, "In the early morning rain, with a dollar in my hand ... with an aching in my heart and my pockets full of sand...."

"Hey!" I yell over his shoulder. "That's a Gordon Lightfoot song."

He grimaces, "No, it isn't. It's Bob Dylan! You don't know Bob Dylan?"

I'm not going to argue — it's a song by Gordon Lightfoot, the great Canadian songwriter. It's his song and it has reached out to me from the other side of the world. Veda sings the phrase, "I'm a long way from home, and I miss my loved ones so ..." and I add the harmony. "In the early morning rain, with nowhere to go!" We both hold onto the last note and burst into laughter. I feel welcomed by the music, by the connection.

Whistling, he turns down a street lined with ancient trees that shade a row of beautiful but rundown colonial mansions. "You want hash? I have very good hash," he offers, "cut with opium?" He adds with delight.

Wow! I've never tried that before ... opium! I remain casual, however. "Ah ... not now, thanks."

"To buy, you want to buy?"

"Ahhhhhhh. No, not now. Thanks."

"Tomorrow, I can meet you tomorrow."

"No, I'm fine. Thanks. I'm not buying just yet, but when I do...."

He shimmies his shoulders and gives it up for now.

Down the road, I see workers, Indian men and women, carrying buckets of cement up a ladder to the top of a wall under construction. An ornate archway dangles over what will become the entrance to an estate. Dozens of tangerine-clad devotees have gathered on the road to witness its installation.

"I have to turn around here," my young driver explains. "They have the road closed all week. The big gates are being delivered tomorrow. I am told they are made of gold!" I can hardly believe that to be true, but he seems so happily convinced that I don't question the possibility.

I pay him a very modest fee and yank my pack out onto the ground. Now I'm really coming undone. Thank goodness for the large safety pin, which is now serving as a mini-curtain rod, securing yards of material in its loop. I can't possibly throw my heavy sack over my shoulder, so I drag it toward the merriment, holding my sari up out of the dust with my other hand.

A tall, handsome Indian man who seems to be in charge, notices me, and smiles. It is possibly the most beautiful smile I have ever seen — his eyes sparkle with playfulness and warmth. I smile back and then stop to watch the final placement of the arch on which the name, Shree Rajneesh Ashram, is prominently carved.

As if on cue, I hear my name, "Annie!" I turn to see Maureen, who now calls herself Gayatri, rushing toward me with her arms open wide. The end of my sari unravels as I run to greet her with a wholehearted hug.

"We've been waiting for you!" she says. "This is perfect timing."

"Did you get my letter?"

"No, but we had a feeling you were on your way. Didn't we, Govinda?"

Her handsome lover glides up beside her, with a wide grin on his face. "Just last night Gayatri said, 'Annie should be here any day now!'" He too embraces me, then grabs my pack, guiding me out of the chaos. "You are coming with us for darshan tonight. We have to get ready."

"Darshan? What's darshan?"

"You're going to meet Rajneesh!" They look me over, now seeing my disarray. My breasts, which are still packed into the tight blouse, are pointing in two different directions. My hair is ratty, and the beautiful sari is trampled and dirty.

"Where'd you buy this sari?" asks Gayatri, amused, gathering it up.

"Bombay. I was so hot."

"Never imagined you in a sari," she teases. "Why didn't you buy orange?"

"Because I do not like orange," I say with conviction. They always bug me about this, like a couple of born-again Christians. They think I should become a sannyasin of Bhagwan Shree Rajneesh.

"I'm here to see you," I insist, "period. For a week at the most." They both laugh, as though they know something I don't.

For years now, they have been travelling back and forth between India and North America, stopping in places in between, buying and selling collectibles and exotic treasures. It doesn't matter what side of the world they are on, they're always the same — happy and loving, graceful and vital.

I am not sure what it means to be a sannyasin, a devotee. It is not important to me, as I am not looking to take a spiritual journey right now. I am on a personal odyssey, wanting to see where my parents and three older brothers lived during the 1930s in India. Mom and Dad were childhood sweethearts, both raised on the Canadian prairies, close to the wilderness. He dreamed of being a doctor, but when he graduated from medical school during the Depression, he couldn't afford to set himself up in practice. He wrote exams for the British Indian Medical Service and was one of a handful of Canadians to be accepted. After studying tropical medicine in London, he was sent to India — Mom had her first son en route to her new home. I imagine that they were quite a distinctive couple amongst the British colonialists during the days of the Raj. They moved several times, in what is now Pakistan, but was India then. My father took a lot of pictures, and I grew up loving the family albums full of extraordinary memories. I particularly loved the picture of my brother's birthday guests happily posed in a huge wagon that was harnessed to a much-decorated camel. As the only child in my family who didn't get to live in such an exotic setting, I've wanted to see these places for myself. I don't intend to stay here for more than a few days.

"Don't you live here at the ashram, with the holy man?" I ask Gayatri, as I scamper down the road, trying to keep up to them.

"No, no. We have a flat with a special nook for guests, like you."

I hear the crowd cheering behind me, and turn to see a large black car with its lights on, slowly approaching the entrance. The handsome gatekeeper motions for the people to clear the road, then glances in my direction. Again, he nods at me distinctly. Gayatri notices.

"See, you've already made an impression. That's Sant. You have good taste."

"I just looked at him. Who wouldn't?" I laugh, retrieving the end of my sari and flinging it around my neck. He is too gorgeous for me, dressed in a soft, peachy silk suit that drapes beautifully over his graceful body as he ushers the big car through the cloud of adoring orange people into the compound. One back window is down, and I catch a glimpse of the guru waving like a king to his subjects.

Gayatri and Govinda, both long and lean, look fabulous in their flowing robes, elegantly edged with embroidered ribbon. Unlike most followers of Rajneesh, they have remained monogamous (I am assuming) and in touch with their families. Other "Rajneeshies" I've talked to believe that enlightenment is not attainable unless you drop all of your attachments — including those you have to people.

Nonattachment has never made sense to me, especially when the teacher and main exponent of this notion drives around in a big car, dressed like a high priest, adorned with gold and precious gems. The word *attachment* must be a metaphor I have not yet grasped. Nobody in this crowd looks detached — except perhaps from obligations.

To remain uncommitted, "like a rolling stone," is a popular moral code these days, and is not limited to gurus and folk singers. I have avoided marriage, going from one man to another, proving to myself, at least, that I am a free woman, independent, able to support myself without help from any man, thank you very much.

On the other hand, I am often lonely. Because of this transient lifestyle, I have learned not to invest emotionally in any relationship because I presuppose it will end without much cause. It has been a long time since I have dated a man who wants to settle down and have a family. Too many lovers have passed through my life. Most of them have remained friends; some of them are now married with children. At times, I have

felt betrayed and confused by them and by myself for resisting the natural urge to be with someone. Why can't I pledge
my trust in anyone?

This easy-come, easy-go rash of relationships and the nonattachment pathway to enlightenment that Rajneesh promotes
are only possible because, for the first time in the history of
humanity, birth control is accessible. Less than ten years ago,
it was not available to unwed women. Good girls like me did
not "go all the way" for many reasons, but pregnancy was the
biggest one. When I was in university, I still thought I had to
be a virgin when I got married. Abortion, like birth control,
was against the law.

Suddenly the pill, the IUD, and the diaphragm were all
there for the asking. I was in my early twenties when I first got
a prescription for the pill, and I remember how remarkable it
was. Suddenly I didn't have to worry about getting pregnant,
which was a good thing — but not totally. I soon realized that
universal birth control liberated men more than it did women.
Sure, it was easier for women to say yes when they weren't
taking such a risk, but it was much harder to say no. It seems
that sex has become a recreational pleasure! I believe that sex
is a beautiful, and possibly, a spiritual experience. What I want
to know is, where is the love now? How is making love different from having sex?

I have learned to take care of myself, by not investing my
heart and soul. And so I've come to realize that it's important
to love your work because if you love your work you can live
without romance.

Or maybe work is the problem. Over the past few years,
I've become tough, decisive, and pretty damned good at my
craft, working seven days a week, putting everything and

everybody else aside. It has changed me. I've become more competitive and less forgiving. While trying to prove myself, I think I have also lost my sense of purpose. I have been so caught up in being as good as "the boys," that I lost my love of making films. As a group, we started out with a strong sense of who we were and who we represented. Then by necessity we focused on making money and building our reputation so we could buy equipment and compete. We won awards and got some recognition. And I know that I got caught up in how cool it is to be a filmmaker rather than how privileged it is to make a difference.

Gayatri and Govinda live on the second floor of an old mansion in Koregan Park. The place is not unlike the ones my folks lived in forty years ago. But they had dozens of servants. It must have been quite an adjustment for my mother, born in 1910, the eldest daughter of a homesteading family that managed to survive out in the middle of the Canadian wilderness. She grew up milking cows, driving a team of horses, growing and canning vegetables, happy with a single present at Christmas, usually handmade.

In India, because she was a memsahib, she was supposed to do nothing. If she boiled the water or swept the porch, for instance, the whole staff would quit, refusing to work for a woman who didn't hold her status. Nellie Rose, who as a child got to order a single pair of shoes from the Eaton's catalogue once a year, suddenly had a dedicated *aya* for each of her three children, plus a gardener, a gateman, maids and cooks, and a personal tailor who sewed outfits for every member of the family for the many social events they attended. She lived in a mansion with wide verandas softened with Persian rugs and tropical fruits that she was not allowed to pick.

I can't help but think of her and Dad as I enter this compound in Pune, which is far past its glory days. The garden has been ignored; the verandas are cluttered with mismatched furniture and laundry. The interior has been divided into several apartments.

But as I climb up the stairs and around the back I come to a place of wonder, eloquently decorated with treasures that Gayatri and Govinda have gathered from around the planet. In a sweet, curtained-off alcove, there's a wooden cot that will be my bed. Outside the window, a mango tree dances in the fast-falling light.

Gayatri reminds me that we're in a rush. I am to shower with a special soap and wear a pure white robe. "When you are with Rajneesh," Gayatri explains, "you cannot smell of anything. So we don't buy the Indian soaps, like the sandalwood I can smell on you now," she cautions. "It is the worst, so hard to wash away. There will be 'sniffers' at the gate. If they smell anything on you, they will refuse you entry."

"Sniffers?" I ask.

"Yes, Govinda is a sniffer sometimes."

"But not tonight," he adds. I struggle to maintain my serious expression while I imagine him like a dog checking people out with his nose.

I'm just going to meet Rajneesh out of curiosity, I tell myself. Then I'm out of here.

The robe is a little long and I look like one of the seven dwarfs, but it's light and cool, much easier to manage than the sari. As I follow Gayatri and Govinda back to the ashram, I try my best to refine my movements as Jyoti taught me earlier today, but I must step quickly to keep up.

There are very few street lights. Huddled forms have already claimed the sidewalks, so we move out onto the street and walk amongst the bikes and smaller vehicles. A bent figure comes at me from behind a tree. The face emerges from the shadows and into focus, looking right at me, disfigured with leprosy, gums exposed to the air, two gaping holes where a nose should be. The voice is liquid and low; her accent beautifully articulated Indian English. "Take pity, memsahib, please, take pity."

I cannot look her in the eyes any longer and thrust an American dollar bill at her. She cannot hold it in her stumpy hands, and it blows across the road. I dart into the traffic and grab it. Quickly, I stuff the bill inside her simple sack and she blesses me, putting her arms in front of her chest. I nod in response. Her face speaks to me of long suffering and intelligence, reminding me that fate can bring misery and is beyond our choosing.

Years ago I met an Irish doctor who was with my father in India. He said Dad used to go out into the villages, that he learned to speak Urdu very well. I wonder if he treated anyone like her. What would he think of me now, rushing off to meet a guru? I doubt I would be here if he were alive. He was a strict father, definite in his opinions. I would have been married with children, I'm sure, like most of my cousins and old friends.

Every evening, about a dozen people are invited to darshan, which is a meeting with Rajneesh, on his veranda. We are the last to arrive and wait at the gate while the people ahead of us are being sniffed. One woman is rejected but refuses to leave and sounds desperate. "You are power-tripping, man, I need to see him. I told you! I am leaving tomorrow. Don't do this to me again!"

A guard pushes her aside, "I can't help what I smell. You smell of onions!"

"I haven't eaten any onions!"

The sniffers move onto the next guest, ignoring her rage. I turn to Gayatri, "Can't the all-powerful Rajneesh tune out the smell of onions?"

"He is very sensitive," she explains seriously. "He doesn't want to be distracted." My scepticism bubbles up, as the woman tries to break through but is blocked. She goes ballistic and is dragged away.

She's probably stoned, I think to myself. Guess I'll pass on the opium-laced hash. How ridiculous is this place? Now I'm getting nervous. I look around for an exit in case I decide to escape.

"Just relax," cautions Govinda. "Don't start to sweat. They'll smell it."

Surprisingly, we are barely sniffed before being given entry. I guess it's because I am with members of the inner circle.

The newly planted garden is verdant and well watered. Vibrant bougainvillea and ginger plants line the cobbled pathways. Walls and fountains are under construction, and I can imagine this becoming a magical oasis in the centre of this dust-choked city.

Pillowed places have been saved for Gayatri and Govinda, and a cushion is quickly found for me. A flute player sets a lofty mood, and a couple of women get up to dance on the glossy floor. The evening birds seem to herald the arrival of Rajneesh as he comes out smiling and settles into a throne-like chair. He seems very casual and a little naughty. By just raising an eyebrow, he initiates a flurry of delight. Everyone titters with anticipation, sensing his greatness and the possibility of witnessing a momentous exchange.

I feel totally dishonest being here. I don't jibe with anyone acting so godlike, so in control over other peoples' lives. Having travelled to Africa and beyond, I am suspicious of all religious leaders; several I've met in the third world openly exploited their exalted powers. At most, I hope to be impressed by a clever teacher.

His gaze falls upon me and I feel exposed. Shyly, cautiously, I briefly smile back as he gives me a warm, loving look. I resist being charmed by his laughing eyes and obvious charisma. It is a long moment before he turns away, seemingly bemused by my lack of response.

I close my eyes and tune in to the music. I am tired and annoyed with myself for agreeing to come here tonight. In so many ways, I have not landed in this time zone yet. I left Canada without much of a plan. The decision was impulsive, a result of wanting to escape, rather than of going somewhere. I left the proverbial pot boiling on the stove back home, thinking I had to get away from it all. And now, forty-eight hours after leaving Edmonton, this.

Whatever "this" is.

His voice is quiet but full of mischief. "Tonight, I welcome the sceptics. I do appreciate the sceptical mind. So please. Go on being sceptical," he says to everyone. "Ask questions for however long it takes. Just see where it gets you!" People laugh. "Believe nothing until you know it. A true sceptic would not listen — even to the Buddha! So be a sceptic, listen only to your own truth."

I swear he is talking to me as I struggle to bat down my innermost thoughts. He holds onto the silence, letting his words sink in, then speaks again.

"You have to sharpen your doubting forces, so that you

can cut through all the rubbish in your mind. All the condi-
tioning. All the falsehoods. All the things you have tried to
be, tried to do — for others. For your own self-gratification.
Your own sense of self-worth. Then...ask the questions which
only you can answer. Nobody else can love on your behalf.
Nobody else can live on your behalf. You decide what it is
you like and what it is you don't like. When you eat, really
taste it; when you listen, really hear it. When you speak,
speak what you believe, not what others have told you. Unless
you discover yourself, there will be no joy, no ecstasy, no
satisfaction."

He says "satisfaction" as though he is Mick Jagger, and
everyone applauds quietly, murmuring their delight. He is so
cool.

One woman, young and childlike, approaches him and
kneels, putting her head to the floor in reverence to him. "You
have a question, Ma?"

She goes to speak, but her voice is weak and tearful. "I
don't know what to do."

"Tell me. What is happening? Hmmm?"

"I am pregnant."

He nods, knowingly. She gathers herself up to continue.
"I'm not ready to have a baby. I don't even know who the father
is." She starts to weep. "I don't want it. Is it wrong to have an
abortion?"

The question shakes me, astonishes me.

I had an abortion — when I was still a teenager. Very few
people know about this. Three, maybe four, people. It has been
my secret, buried so deeply that I rarely think of it anymore,
but here it is, kicked to the surface after having been buried
beneath layers of guilt and self-loathing for more than ten

years. The past comes bubbling up from the pit of my stomach, and I feel as though I am going to retch.

Rajneesh is nonchalant in his answer.

"There is no question here. When a baby is born, a mother must be born. If you do not want to be a mother, then do not have the child. It's a wonderful experience to be a mother; for most women, the most wondrous experience. *But,* if you choose not to be a mother, the soul will choose another mother. It is your ego that thinks you have such a great power here, that this decision is going to be measured by the great gods of the universe. What will they think of you? Do you think they are all watching you? Judging you? Really? That is a fantasy. Like a Walt Disney movie. Listen. You cannot kill a soul. Everything of the flesh grows old and dies of the flesh. But the soul! The soul goes on! Your own soul will go on!

"Life is precious. Do not get me wrong. I love life. Don't misunderstand me. I am not saying that this loss — of a great possibility — is not a loss. But if every child is a wanted child, then there is hope for this world. I am optimistic that this new freedom of choice will lead to a more enlightened world."

Suddenly he looks directly at me. "This was a good question, yes?"

He's asking me?

"Yes," I stammer. He must have seen me flinch. Or did he see my fascination in his response. I am stupefied by the serendipity at play here, convinced now that he can hear my innermost thoughts. He laughs.

"And you are Gayatri and Govinda's friend? Yes?"

"Yes, I didn't expect to be here tonight. They invited me. I shouldn't have come...." I blabber on, like someone who has wandered into the wrong bathroom. Everyone laughs, including me. I don't know why.

"You make us laugh. Come closer here. Come sit with me."

I resist. "Don't waste your time on me. These people have prepared their questions. I am just visiting." Everyone laughs again. Why? What is this joke they share? Can they hear the panic in my voice?

"Come. Come closer."

Everyone waits.

Put on the spot, I shuffle forward a little. "Yes, yes," he encourages me, "good. Come right here, in front of me, don't be so nervous." He beckons me with his hands reassuringly. "I have never hurt anyone."

Reluctantly, I get closer and closer to his laughing eyes. I look long and hard at him. He nods, "You will be a sannyasin, yes?"

"Ah, no, no, no, no," I rattle off. "I am not here for that ... I am not ready for anything like —"

ZAP!

What was that?!?

He touched me on my forehead, between the eyes, with his finger, and a buzz of something surged through my body. It felt warm and electric. I am awash with pleasure, dizzy with the surprise of it all. I have lost my composure. I sit there, mouth open, stunned. Have I been hypnotized? Am I delirious? I am so tired, yet so awake. I cannot escape the twinkle of his eyes.

"You will be Mugdha. Ma Deva Mugdha. Do you know what that means?" I can only shake my head. "You remember the feeling you had when you fell in love — for the very first time?" I nod. I was fourteen. He chuckles. "Well, that is mugdha. Totally committed, without question. Madly in love. And Deva? Well Deva can be the Devil or the Divine. So you are madly in love with the Devil and the Divine. Good name, yes?"

It is much more interesting than Anne, for certain. Gayatri and Govinda nod approvingly. My rebellious mind is still trying to figure out how he did what he did. It was not my imagination — I know it was real. It overwhelmed me. Did he have some kind of battery-operated buzzer in his hand? I watch him gesture gracefully, his hand and arms waving with expression. I see no trick. He doesn't have a magic wand. Perhaps, he is the magic wand.

He leans into me. "You will stay in Pune, Ma Deva Mugdha, for just a little while, with us. Just stop and smell the roses, yes? Get yourself back on course. Everything else can wait."

I am so stunned, I can only nod.

I could stay. What harm could come of it? I am disenchanted with my life. Gayatri and Govinda have been with him for several years and it hasn't done them any harm. In fact, I admire, even envy them. They appear to have a loving and worriless outlook on life.

Maybe this is where I belong. Like so many others here, I have been a wanderer, looking for something beyond the obvious patterns of our society. I haven't gotten married, nor have I latched onto a demanding or lucrative career. Why, I'm not sure. I know that the early death of my father left me in shock. Then becoming pregnant at nineteen wiped out my innocent fantasies about sex and love being one and the same.

I am confounded by Rajneesh's discourse on abortion! The truth, I realize now, is that I was raped. But nobody asked me how it happened. "The less said, the better" was the code of the day. So I hid it. I don't think I even knew or uttered the word, *rape*.

But I have, at times, felt like a slut, a disappointment, unworthy of being loved, guilty of murder perhaps. Rajneesh's response is so contrary to what I was taught to believe that I can't immediately embrace it — even though it would be a convenient way to shed my burden of shame. I rarely go to church, but I'm still conditioned, I guess, by the Christian code that would judge me. In the church's eyes, I have committed murder. I was weak and wicked. I killed my own child. I know many people who believe that — people who lived on the same block as me. I could never look them in the eye after what I did.

Still, religion continued to intrigue me. I was always a seeker of sorts. As a teenager, I was curious to find God. I tried every Christian denomination (that being the only religion I knew of) in the city, hoping one of them would diminish my doubts about the Messiah. I couldn't bring myself to believe in the Virgin Birth or the Resurrection. I thought the parables were brilliant, so were the Ten Commandments. "Love thine enemy" was a real test of humility. If the world could just embrace a few simple precepts like "Do unto others as you would have them do unto you," then peace would be possible.

But I cannot believe that The Almighty is watching over each and every one of us. Hopefully Rajneesh will offer up something more credible, more profound. Something we can all embrace. My hopes are not high, but I am motivated to stay and hear more.

February 13, 1976
Dear Mom,
Pune is a beautiful little colonial city with a polo club and a
racetrack much like the ones in your photographs. Very British.
I have decided to stay here for a while. Maureen has some
wonderful friends, and I have found an apartment to rent by
the week. Don't worry about me.
Love, your daughter, Anne

HAVING NOTHING ORANGE to wear, Gayatri takes me to her
tailor, Omari. With the arrival of so many Westerners, the
Pune fabric stores are packed with new bolts of fabulous cloth
in every shade of orange, from red to yellow. Within a day, I
have a new wardrobe — three monk-like robes and five salwar
kameez, the versatile Indian suits for women, perfect for me.
Made to measure, the tunic flatters my full figure, and with
the baggy pants I can do cartwheels in public if that is my
pleasure. Omari has used a generous amount of flowing silk
so I can indulge in the sweet sway of the fabric when I walk.

I find a room at the Diamond Hotel and pay up for a
couple of weeks. Rajneesh is about to begin a series of lec-
tures in English, on the Ten Bulls of Taoism, a series of short
poems used in the Zen tradition to describe the journey
toward Enlightenment.

The First Bull of Tao — In Search of The Bull
In the pasture of the world, I endlessly push aside the tall
grasses in search of the Ox.
Following unnamed rivers, lost upon the interpenetrating
paths of distant mountains,
My strength failing and my vitality exhausted,
I cannot find the Ox.

EVERY DAY, BEFORE DAWN, the streets of Koregan Park fill up with sannaysins gravitating toward the ashram. Sant is there to open the gate (gilded with brass, not gold), and greets me with a glowing smile, "Good morning, Ma Deva Mugdha."

"Good morning, Sant!"

I am surprised that he knows my name. He must have asked somebody.

Silently, I enter Buddha Hall, which isn't actually a hall yet. Presently, it is a large shiny cement floor surrounded by temporary walls made of bamboo, with wooden scaffolding and a ceiling of draped cloth that glimmers in the morning light. Indian musicians, nestled together in a carpeted corner, tune their instruments. A few foreigners, excited to be included, join them with a variety of acoustic stringed instruments, flutes, and drums from the far corners of the planet.

I lay out my mat, which defines my personal space, in preparation for the morning meditation. It is understood that "anything goes, as long as you stay on your mat."

This is the *dynamic meditation*, otherwise known as the *madness meditation*. It takes several days for me to grasp the sequence, which is complicated by the fact that we are all blindfolded. As we settle ourselves, securing the scarves around our heads, blacking out the world, the drummers begin to mark out a heavy primal beat, giving us the signal to begin.

We begin with chaotic breathing — through the nose. We're told to focus on the exhalation, which I find tricky, but I do my best. The idea is to infuse our bodies with as much oxygen as possible. This first stage takes about ten minutes, but it feels like forever.

Finally the music shifts into a higher gear, signalling me to seek out my insanity. Following whatever thoughts are racing through my mind, I am charged to pursue my own madness. I chase down anger, remorse, greed, joy, sadness, desire, fear — memories born of times I have forgotten. Raging on until I am truly barmy, I mourn my father's death, I rant at old friends and lovers, I rejoice in the freedom of being here, I convulse with outrageousness, I beat myself up for being fat and ugly. Emotions explode inside me, as I lose all control, resisting the need to censor myself, leaping into the unknown. It's like a dress rehearsal for death, or a trip on acid, or self-induced insanity. I lose sense of time and I forget where I am. The point, of course, is to *lose one's mind*.

The meditation falls apart if I stop and question why I am doing this. One must not think. One must just do. There are no answers. My inner cowgirl refuses to stay quiet: This is absolute nonsense, a ridiculous game thought up by a madman. Get the hell out of here before you are brainwashed!

During the meditation, some participants do get lost. I cannot see them, of course, but I can hear them, going out of control, leaving their mat, screaming and crying. Sometimes the music dwindles to silence while designated guards rush in to bring the madness under control, and we stand there, suspended, wet with sweat, wondering who it might be. It could have been me — off my rocker, as my mother would say. It is so bizarre. Impossible to explain to anyone who hasn't been here.

The music changes again. We all jump up, throwing our hands in the air and shouting "Hoo! Hoo! Hoo! Hoo!" over and over. Together our voices crescendo, creating an overwhelming emotional pulse. "Hoo! Hoo! Hoo! Hoo!" To a stranger, we might appear like a bunch of baboons in heat — eagerly jumping higher and higher, yelling louder and louder.

It's exhausting; it goes on and on, testing my limits. I give it my all — anything less and the exercise is pointless.

I am wet with sweat when the music evolves, slowing down, becoming lyrical and fluid. Flutes play against gently plucked strings as voices embellish melodies that weave together with a sense of discovery and joyfulness. Still blindfolded, I am uninhibited. I dance and sing, my thoughts drifting away, reacting spontaneously to the musicians, who in turn follow their own instincts. The music is enchanting, full of discovery. Each person is autonomous, in his or her own bubble, protected from judgment or the pressure of expectations. Like a whirling dervish, I spin and lose myself amongst the vibrations — soaking up the moments of magic. It could be a path to enlightenment — but I'm not there yet.

Then, at last, silence. I drop to the ground, my energy completely spent. With no idea of what others are doing, I lie there listening. I reach for the sound that is furthest away — a train, a horn, a church bell, a bird call. Then I pull my attention closer, closer and closer, bringing my awareness into the surrounding environment, listening to the cool breeze, the people breathing in the room, the footsteps and the sighs, closer and closer until all I can hear is my own heartbeat. Concentrating, I slow it down until it is beating out an easy, peaceful tempo as I balance on the edge of consciousness. Yes, this is the way, I tell myself; I will continue on this path. I will listen to Rajneesh and do as he tells me to do.

The Second Bull of Tao — Discovery of The Footprints
Along the riverbank under the trees, I discover footprints,
Even under the fragrant grass, I see his prints,
Deep in remote mountains they are found.
These traces can no more be hidden than one's nose, looking heavenward.

WE REMAIN IN SILENCE until the gong rings. Perhaps some have emptied their minds — I am usually lost in some internal musings.

The dynamic meditation takes about an hour, after which there is time for tea before we funnel into the garden for the morning discourse. Rajneesh sits on his veranda with his chosen few around him. Several tall, strong men stand guard at the entrances, mostly Indians, which reminds me that recent attempts have been made on our guru's life. His untraditional methods and teachings have provoked outrage amongst many.

To my mind, he is provocative, in a good way. He titillates his listeners through wit and humour, weaving different wisdoms together, showing how they are the same, how they complement each other. They all say the same things. The illusive experience, the moment of oneness, is there for all of us. He is full of surprises and contradictions, telling jokes, teasing us all. I can see why so many people have gathered around him. The whole world can laugh, can appreciate from his insights. Especially when it comes to tantric sex.

"In the deepest moment of lovemaking, thinking stops and you can feel the life force, the pulse and nothing else. The moment is so intriguing, the moment so tremendously powerful, so intense, so alive that you are absorbed by it. You are simply in awe. A great wonder holds you for just that moment. This is the closest that most people get to being totally aware, totally present. The great challenge is to sustain this moment. You can do it with a partner or you can do it on your own. It is possible. Yes, you can bring yourself to a euphoric state and sustain it ... but as soon as the little voice speaks up — the little voice, you know the little voice in your head ... the moment is gone. Yes?"

Some mornings, he accepts questions, but I never ask any because he always seems to address what is on my mind. He is anti-religion and says, "God is the greatest lie created by mankind." People are like children, he explains. "They want a father, a mother to take over, to make the decisions when they are afraid, in trouble, or sick. They call out for help — but there is no father in Heaven. That is an illusion. There is no God, or Goddess, but there is *godliness*. Yes. Godliness is within each and every living thing."

The Third Bull of Tao — Perceiving the Bull
I hear the song of the nightingale.
The sun is warm, the wind is mild, willows are green along the shore —
Here no Ox can hide!
What artist can draw that massive head, those majestic horns?

THE COMMUNITY IS GROWING so quickly. Now you have to book at least a week ahead for darshan. There are no last-minute invitations. The main floor of the house has become a maze of busy offices, and the second floor is being used for encounter groups. Psychologists are coming from all over the world to work under the Master's guidance.

I attended some Gestalt therapy groups back home. The leaders were all men with big egos. During one weekend retreat, (a group I took for a university psychology course credit) I experienced the leader, a professor, use his position of power. He was a good-looking charmer and almost everyone opened up to him, trusted him with their intimacies. He moved in on the three most attractive women — one was shy and naïve; the second had done two previous groups with him and was smitten; and the third was going through a divorce and shared her feelings of rejection. He teased and flirted with these three so blatantly that a couple of the young men called him on it. But he skilfully turned their complaints back on them, brutal in his defence. The young men retreated. He continued his games with the women, ignoring the rest of us. Eventually I did try to confront him, but it got ugly and humiliating very quickly. He didn't own his behaviour, and I was afraid I would lose my credits so I sat back and watched the competition. In the end, I believe he bonked two of them but no one reported him. He left a trail of bewildered students and one broken heart in his wake.

Disenchanted by that experience, I decided that the guru wannabes arriving at the ashram were nothing but trouble. I planned to get out of here before more of them arrived and I was pressured to participate.

When I arrived in Pune a few weeks ago, there were a couple of hundred Westerners and many more Indians. Since then, the balance has shifted dramatically. New devotees pour in from Europe, Asia, and the Americas. Many dress immodestly, flaunting their promiscuity and self-declared liberation causing more tensions between the locals and the ashram. Traditions are held strong here. Unmarried women who are not virgins are worthless. Many marriages in India are arranged when the future bride and groom are still children. Romantic films are a very popular form of entertainment, but actors are not allowed to kiss on screen. Local Indian businesses are making money from this explosion of foreign visitors, but others would rather see Rajneesh dead.

Most evenings, I return to the ashram to make merry with the musicians, singers, and dancers who perform for Bhagwan after darshan. I love that these soulmates from all over the world have landed here to share in this alchemy. Sometimes I drum or dance, but mostly I sing, riffing off whatever is happening, improvising a descant or a harmony. There is one voice that I recognize from the morning meditation, a clear high voice that blends so well with my own. We find each other, first by listening, then by sight. She is Dutch and her sannyasin name is Vipassana. Both of us blonde, we look like sisters and are sometimes mistaken for each other. Together we are challenged by the Indian singers who break open the tempered scales and encourage us to throw away our need for tonality and keys. They are not bound to the tempered scale of twelve separate tones like we are. They melodically slide up and down in pitch, playing on the passion that builds and subsides, multiple times, orgasmic in nature. The rhythm volleys back and forth with the tabla players and the singers, who use their voices like plucked strings for rapid exchanges. It is mind-boggling as we try to emulate the intricacies, dividing the rhythms into five, or seven, or twenty-three, and beyond. There is no room for thinking; one can only mindlessly echo their phrases.

One night, at the height of such rapture, I see Sant watching me. It's hard to believe he has singled me out of this collection of beautiful people. He smiles at me and I nod back, bewitched.

Ah ... this feeling ... Mugdha, the feeling for which you are named! Madly in love ... with the Divine! He does take my breath away with his smile and his steady gaze. His presence distracts me, so for fun I turn and sing to him like I'm in some musical or Indian movie. He laughs and embraces my performance as a gift.

The Fourth Bull of Tao — Catching the Bull
I seize him with a terrific struggle.
His great will and power are inexhaustible.
He charges to the high plateau far above the cloud-mists,
Or in an impenetrable ravine he stands.

WORDLESSLY, Sant and I leave together. He is Sikh by birth. I have read about the Sikhs, the great warriors. My father marched out of India with the Ninth Indian Division in 1941, which made me curious about this history. We go to a restaurant unfamiliar to me. Everyone there knows him and we are immediately served. Finally, he speaks. "Do you like your food spicy?"

"Yes, I do." End of conversation.

After we eat, I ask a few questions. His English is limited but proper and formal. "I have been with Bhagwan since the beginning," he tells me. "He was my professor, I was his student. I knew immediately that he would be my Master."

He seems so authentic compared to the cocky Westerners who pose as sages, putting themselves above the others. Some are boastful; many of them are elitist, contradicting what is being taught here. How can you boast about being humble?

In some ways, the ashram feels like high school, with the "in group" that gets to be close to the Master and the loners who sit off to the side, hoping to be included. Sant doesn't try to win favour with anyone; he just is. Being with him is easy. Being with him convinces me to extend my stay.

My hotel is a rundown, rat-infested building with a tired facade of faded grandeur, featuring large, ornate balconies. Fifty years ago, this was a popular colonial hotel, boasting an impressive ballroom with a stunning mosaic floor and a decorative ceiling. Now the ballroom is like a barn, divided into stalls or cubicles to accommodate the flood of low-budget travellers. Each cubicle has a small, lockable door and walls, but no ceiling. It is just big enough for a small bed, a chair, and a cheap, boxy wardrobe. The air in the great room is usually heavy with hash smoke and Nag Champa incense, while the music is loud, mixing East with West amidst the moans of copulating couples as they attempt to reach and sustain nirvana.

Tonight, I am happy that Sant says good night to me in the garden with a tender kiss. I have hosted a few forgettable partners in my cubicle; I did not reach nirvana.

March 2, 1976
Dear Mom, Got your letter, delivered to the hotel. Thanks.
Glad you have moved from that noisy apartment. Maureen is
travelling back to Canada and is going to bring a few things
from me to you. The antique market here is fascinating.
I found an ornate silver box housing a bridge set of cards
complete with score pad and pencil. Also an antique polo
mallet with an engraved handle — I love the image of Dad,
the cowboy doctor, playing polo with his cronies here —
Polo is still quite popular but the horses look a little
underweight!
Love to everyone. Anne

RAJNEESH HAS BEEN in the news — there have been more threats to his life. The number of guards at the ashram has doubled, but the gates are still open. Laxmi, the woman who manages the place, has bought the property next door, another old mansion. She is very straightforward in her dealings.

I've heard she was a businesswoman in her former life, which fits. The walls in between the two properties are coming down so that the grounds will double in size. New toilets from Europe are being installed in the old house, and a vegetarian restaurant is opening in the compound. With all the renovations and the new paint, this place is unrecognizable from how it was when I landed here. Dozens of new people arrive every day, looking like excited children entering a candy shop. (Oddly, there are few "real" children amongst us — followers are discouraged from bringing them into the community.)

Apparently, the ashram is getting a lot of press abroad. The enthusiasm and joyfulness is contagious, but quietly, down deep, I remain a sceptic. Yes, I get caught up in the magic, but I'm not selling my house just yet.

My second darshan is different from the first. I miss Gayatri and Govinda, who are gone now, on their annual trading trip. Rajneesh takes a few questions, but it is not an intimate exchange like the one I had only weeks ago. There is not as much banter between him and his followers. I am left longing for that special one-to-one moment. People dance and sing for him, which is beautiful, and before we leave he does address a few of us briefly, assigning us to the new groups being offered. I'm not sure that he recognizes me as Mugdha, but he does direct me specifically: "You will take the Om Marathon! Four days — non-stop. It will liberate you from yourself," he promises. "Risk everything!"

I don't want to do any groups. Honestly. But how can I refuse? I mean I can, but then what would be the point of being here if I don't take his direction? The "world" seems comfortably far away. I like that. I like my name. It's happening, I think. I am finding my inner grace.

The Om Marathon is expensive but I can swing it if I cancel my trip to Karachi, which means giving up my original quest to visit my parents' former home. I will have to come back to India some other time. The group leader has a reputation for being tough and brutally honest, which is good. I can do "brutally honest," but it will be a challenge to "surrender" my ego — maybe this resistance is exactly what I should confront. I will take the risk.

We gather in what was once a bedroom on the second floor of the big house. It's hot and musty, with a ceiling fan stirring up the stale smell. The leader comes in and we are simply told, "Get naked and put your clothes away. You are not going to need them."

My inner cowgirl saddles up. "For God's sake, woman, get out of here! This man is a pervert, a power sucker! You don't need this!" I almost take her advice.

I hate my body. My boobs are too big, my legs too short, my figure too curvy. I have always felt like the ugliest girl in my extended family, my mother being the beauty amongst us all. To put it mildly, being naked in front of a roomful of strangers is totally diminishing.

Most of the men just go for it and throw their clothes in a corner. Every part of me wants to get out of here now.

Instead, I strip down, feeling sick to my stomach, and attempt to hold on to my robe, covering myself. It is quickly taken away by the leader's assistant.

Then we sit in a circle, as directed.

Some of the men find this exciting and can't keep their "reactions" under control. I'm glad I'm not a guy! I am slightly aroused, yes, but mostly I'm on the defensive. If anybody tries to touch me, my claws will come out!

All of us have sannyasin names. I know nothing about anyone; they know nothing about me. They tell us that after a few days our "true nature" will be exposed. It's like being in a war — it will bring out the best and worst in all of us.

The smell of nervous sweat permeates the room but mostly I smell my own stink. "Liberate myself from myself" becomes my silent mantra. I want to drop this feeling of shame I have felt throughout my life — it holds me down. It holds me back.

The Fifth Bull of Tao — Taming the Bull
The whip and rope are necessary,
Else he might stray off down some dusty road.
Being well-trained, he becomes naturally gentle.
Then, unfettered, he obeys his master.

AS A PERSON WHO IS confused and uncertain about what I am going to do with the rest of my life, I am perfect fodder for a group like this. I am open to suggestion, willing to try almost anything, answerable to no one. If I decide to stay at the ashram indefinitely, no one will come looking for me because no one depends on me, except my mother to a point, but even she has remarried and is self-sufficient. I have a little house I could sell and that would be enough money for me to stay here for the rest of my life if I so decided. My disappearance would soon be absorbed. Why not avoid the stress of a career, a family, the bills, and the middle-class responsibilities that could suck away at my freedom and my soul?

After doing some stretches and chanting, the real work begins. The leader tells me to stand up in front of the others. Why me!?!

I get up, trying, with utter futility, to do it gracefully, holding my hand over my crotch.

He instructs the others, "Look at Ma Deva Mugdha and say, out loud, what you see. The first thing that comes to mind."

The group doesn't hold back. Words spill out of them spontaneously. "Kind — tough — hard — frightened — sad — funny — smart — ashamed — angry — masculine — dishonest — ugly — weak — brave."

The leader urges them on, "Come on, everyone! Dig in! Look deeper! Don't censor yourself!"

The words come at me like bullets. "Aggressive — arrogant — shy — bitchy — bitter — lost — fat — stupid — disgusting." I try to control my reaction to this battery of insults, but it's not easy. I try influencing them with my facial expressions — I am amused, I am smiling, I am incredulous, I am hurt — but they keep shooting me down.

The words get meaner. "Spiteful — slut — lazy — pig — wimp — liar — deadbeat." And so it goes until they cannot think of any more words.

I feel beaten up and alone. Paralyzed. Powerless. No one tries to defend me. What in hell am I doing here? What kind of bullshit exercise is this? I retreat to a corner, ready to lambaste the next attacker, my hands in tight fists.

The leader seems pleased with the exercise, like everybody got it right. "Very good," he says, smiling like a happy dad. "The words you used to describe Mugdha have nothing to do with her. They have everything to do with you. It's about how you see yourself in her — you have no idea who she is. So it's time to own what you said. Let's explore how you really feel about yourself."

He turns to me. "Did you find that exercise upsetting?"

"No," I lie.

"Anyone believe her?" he asks.

Nobody believes me. They challenge me, shaking their heads. I smile, "Okay, yes. But only because some of it is true. I am kind and brave and a bit shy." Some of them see the humour. Others call me on it. "Actually," I add, "I am all of those things — and that's why it stung." The leader likes that I get it — he chose the right person to start things off. He is all puffed up thinking he is just so good at what he does.

We eat and sleep in this room. There's a water closet down the hall, with a tap, and a bucket for flushing. We get smellier, more emotional, and less defensive. I do not hold back; it gets physical but this is no orgy. It builds to a sequence of cathartic outbursts, with people exposing their anger and hurt and trying to take it out on other members of the group. Having come from a family that never showed their emotions, it is the first time I am pushed to lose my temper. My gut-wrenching words fly out of my mouth without thought. I can't remember what I said, but in the end, I do feel as though I have survived something that has changed me. My emotions are a part of me, not to be denied. And I don't apologize for how I look or smell or feel about anybody. I am who I am. We are all complex individuals, with experiences, good and bad, that have shaped us. Nothing is personal; there are no secrets. I have come out knowing myself better and am more able to accept my strengths and weaknesses. I'm not perfect, but I'm worth keeping. I forgive myself completely for disappointing my parents, for having had an abortion, for everything and anything ... I feel ready to move on.

The Sixth Bull of Tao — Riding the Bull Home
Mounting the Ox, slowly I return homeward.
The voice of my flute intones through the evening.
Measuring with hand-beats the pulsating harmony,
I direct the endless rhythm.
Whoever hears this melody will join me.

SO MANY PEOPLE come to the morning meditation now, that there is no room in the hall for the live musicians. Now we move to a recording that is played loudly over inadequate speakers — it's not the same but still incredible with maybe a thousand seekers in attendance.

A fancy boutique now sells books, pictures, music cassettes, odourless soap, and of course, beads, jewellery, and orange clothing. It is certainly the most beautiful shop in Pune, with lovely places to sit and contemplate how much to spend.

Being seen with Sant puts me closer to the centre of what's happening. Without making any effort, I am included, I am somebody. Wary and reticent around those who are suddenly friendly but don't know me, I eat with my Indian sannyasin friends when I can, so that I can see what is happening through their eyes. It appears to me that there is a mutual admiration society, with the more established members hugging and loving and smiling at each other. They are blessed, feeling chosen and grateful that they have found their master. I feel more comfortable amongst those who stay in the shadows, and find a few close friends.

It is not uncommon for Indians to dedicate themselves to a spiritual life, but Rajneesh is not a typical guru. Some of Sant's friends have been disowned by their families for having made the decision to follow Rajneesh. If I turn up back home

calling myself Mugdha and wearing orange, I might be disowned, too. But that does not concern me. I feel no need to
please, or impress, or prove myself right. It will be an interesting test of friendship and acceptance. Why should I care if
people judge me for something that really has no impact on
their lives?

Laxmi has heard from Sant that I make films and calls me
in to have a talk with her. She is making plans to produce and
distribute videos of Bhagwan's discourses. She asks me what
I think of video.

"Well," I tell her, "I have worked with it and have found it
frustrating. The equipment is bulky, and if it breaks down it's
hard to find someone who can fix it. It needs to be kept clean,
which would be a challenge in this dusty city. The technology
is very new and changing so quickly, that what you buy now
will soon be obsolete. Personally, I would stick with film until
video becomes more advanced — and standardized."

Laxmi keeps nodding, looking at me. "You have won
awards, yes?"

"Yes. Some."

"Where?"

"The most impressive one, I guess, would be the Blue
Ribbon at the New York Documentary Film Festival."

She nods and shimmies her shoulders some more. "What
was that film about?"

"It was about women ... the history of pioneer women in
Canada."

She is surprised but pleased. "Good, good. We need you."

I'm not anxious to get involved and I think she might be
playing with me. So I tell her what I know. "I met some of
the sannyasins who are keen on video. They said that you

encouraged them to find out what is the best video set-up on the market right now and to make a list so you can purchase it. They were very excited."

"Yes. I think video is very good," she tells me. "They shot one of Bhagwan's discourses and then showed it to me the same day!"

"Well, this is it's great advantage — you don't need to go to a laboratory."

She agrees. "And we are installing bigger screens so that we can project to thousands of people at a time while he is speaking. You can do that now with these cameras."

I am honest. "Video is meant for small screens ... on a large screen the image will go soft and out of focus. I am sure it will get better, but right now it is substandard. Television networks, for example, will not air it." This last point registers with her.

I can see a power structure crystallizing around Rajneesh, and Laxmi is his chief of staff. Many sannyasins are very ambitious; they want to be close to him, to photograph him, to guard him, to transcribe and edit the discourses, to design the book jackets, and so on. The problem is, *he* may be enlightened, but nobody else I've met here is. On occasion, Rajneesh will declare that someone has reached Nirvana and there is a great flurry of excitement. It's as though someone has won a championship. Something about it doesn't sit well with me. It seems contrary to everything he says. Actually, he often contradicts himself.

And now this production of videos is another way to gain access to the man himself. Who will get to shoot them, direct them? Who will set the style, the pace, the standard? Whoever it is will have access to Rajneesh directly on a daily basis and will win a place in the inner circle.

I think the still photographers have done sterling work; they have obvious skills and their photos are brilliant. Video should be an extension of their domain. "I don't want to take anyone's place," I tell Laxmi.

"You are not taking anyone's place. You are a film director. We need you. We are going to build a library of films. We will distribute them all over the world. This is a serious undertaking. And you, Ma, will do your best work under Bhagwan. This is your destiny."

If Rajneesh personally asks me to do this, I will do my best, but the situation is beginning to feel eerily similar to the one I left months ago. I find myself too accommodating in a group. I hate trying to second-guess everyone — it sparks an old need to please. I promise Laxmi that I will think about it and give her an answer soon. But in my heart of hearts, I want to fly solo.

Nobody understands my reluctance, especially Sant. I could stay here and be creative for as long as I want. Rajneesh will have an impact on the whole world, and I'll have considerable influence over how he is presented. Rajneesh, even with all of his contradictions, has a huge following, and it's growing.

March 20, 1976
Dear Mom,
Sorry I have not written sooner. Hope you received the gifts from Maureen. I am still in Pune, where I might take a job. I am still planning to meet up with my friend Cheryl in Bangkok next month, but after that I might come back here. Don't worry about me. I am having a most interesting time. Much love, Anne

PEOPLE NOW WRITE DOWN questions for darshan and hand them in on folded paper — it's like a game I played as a child. Rajneesh reads one of them out loud. "Dear Bhagwan, what do you want to happen here?"

Rajneesh laughs. "I want you all to find your own happiness. You don't need anyone but yourself. No prayer. No priest. You alone are enough to face the sunrise. You don't need somebody to interpret it for you. You are here, every individual is here; the wonder of existence is here. Be silent and be aware. There is no need for any religion, for any god, for any organization that will control. It is up to the individual to be aware and to be loving. Be happy. It's up to you. Love is a state of being, not a relationship."

I am sitting beside Sant. Rajneesh looks at us and smiles. I wonder if he knows we are together sometimes. Then he motions to me, which is a surprise, as he has not really acknowledged me since my first darshan.

"You ... come closer please." Oh no, he's going to put me in charge of the video department. I can't do it. I'll have to decline.

But no. "I think this is a very good time for you to go into silence. Right now. Right here. For four days, okay? No talking. No singing. And then. You come back and we will talk, yes?"

I go to speak. "Ah!" He stops me, and I laugh. "No laughing either, Ma. Silence, beginning now." I nod obediently.

Silence is a gift. Alone, I wander into the back streets of the city. Throwing my dupatta (long scarf) over my head and hiding my face, I disappear. Now I walk slowly and effortlessly, with grace, even though most of the time I am lost. It doesn't matter to me; there is nowhere I should be. I love being alone and quiet. I know that, at some point, I'll come to the end of the road. There's no need to think beyond the present.

The Seventh Bull of Tao — The Bull Transcended
Astride the Ox, I reach home.
I have abandoned the whip and ropes.
I am serene. The Ox too can rest. The dawn has come.
In blissful repose,
Within my thatched dwelling.

I AM SHOCKED to hear that my Dutch singing friend is very ill. It has happened so quietly. Her brother, who is also a sannyasin, took her to Bombay, I am told, where she was diagnosed with a malignant brain tumour. Now she lies, unconscious, in a Pune hospital. Within days, we are told she is dying.

Bhagwan urges us to be with her, to go to her bedside, and to witness this silent departure. It's a long walk away, but there is a flow of orange people coming and going from the hospital. The hallway is clogged with people waiting their turn to visit her. I find a place against the wall and watch. Being in silence, I feel invisible. Her brother and close friends — those who speak her language and know her birth name — stay in the room with her. I am close enough to see inside whenever the door opens, which becomes increasingly infrequent.

As evening descends, a few of the musicians I know arrive and play. I cannot sing — but I add to the hushed rhythm beneath the soft chanting that is reaching out to her subconscious. She lies still, her head wrapped in white cloth. The music ebbs and flows — until there is silence.

The day she dies, darshan is cancelled and we are all called to hear Rajneesh speak. He wants us to celebrate Vipassana's death. "It's a high death — she died without a struggle," he says, "and when you do it that way, only one more death is possible."

Where does the idea of high deaths and low deaths come from? Who sorted all that out? Who decided when a death is auspicious? It seems as though all religions are run by men who put up obstacles, install gates on the mythical road to Enlightenment, or Heaven, or Everlasting Life of some kind. That way they are able to control all of those who wish to journey with them. Such imaginations these men have! I thought Rajneesh was anti-religion, but this sounds very religious to me.

But when Rajneesh says this, I do connect: "We must meet death with our eyes open. Experience the last moment. Watch death happen. Be there when it happens. That is the ultimate challenge — the most important. Do not fear it. Experience it with total awareness."

We are told she must be cremated within a day of death. The body is washed and dressed for the cremation. Some of us come in before the procession and adorn Vipassana's body with flowers. My period of silence is over, so I will sing with the others in the procession, as she is carried through the streets of the city to the funeral pyre near the river. We follow the drums and chant, "Govinda, Bolo hari, Gopala, Bolo." She sang this mantra in the garden only weeks ago. It feels surreal that her body is being carried, floating above our heads, looking peaceful and sublime.

The ceremony just happens. With death so omnipresent in India, the rituals take over, and everything unfolds without any clear leader. For thousands of years, the same traditions have shaped the lives and deaths of the people, and this makes me feel that I am a part of a bigger evolution — a natural rhythm that will continue to repeat itself until the end of time.

Vipassana's voice crossed over mine many times in harmony — I can hear her voice in mine now. Could she have imagined this cadence to her life?

It is dusk when we reach the funeral pyre. Her brother and friends place her body upon the wood that has been stacked like a waiting cradle. More wood is added to build the fire up and over her. From a distance, I see Vipassana's brother being instructed on how to carry out the last rites. It appears that they are placing some small items around her head and sprinkling ghee over her body and over the wood before lighting the fire. I strain to see it all, slightly ashamed of my morbid curiosity.

The chanting and drumming continues as the fire turns into a roaring blaze. Black smoke spirals into the air; ashes descend on us like confetti. I feel the soot on my skin, sticky and oily. The smell of burnt meat and hair causes some to leave, some to retch. It makes me cough and I cover my face. Her glowing body seems to levitate within the inferno. Her skull becomes a brilliant red orb. Her brother is given a long bamboo spear by one of the elders. Suddenly, he thrusts the pointed end into the skull and it explodes into a ball of fire shooting upwards.

Her soul has been released from its earthly domain.

The Eighth Bull of Tao — Both Bull and Self Transcended
Whip, rope, person, and Ox — all merge in No Thing.
This heaven is so vast, no message can stain it.
How may a snowflake exist in a raging fire?
Here are the footprints of the Ancestors.

WE ALL STAND THERE, watching, in silence. A shared flash of wakefulness. It is the greatest lesson — beyond words, beyond thought.

I stay until the fire is finished. A few people stay to retrieve the charred bones that remain.

As I wander back to my hotel, Sant catches up to me and says nothing. There is nothing to say. The event has shifted my perception of life; death is so close and so real now. Like love, you can talk about it, you can name it, but it is not real until you experience it. Death remains the unknown for all of us, but now I accept its inevitability. Tonight, it snuck up and almost knocked me over. I am reeling from the impact and inwardly finding a new balance.

I did not see my father's dead body. He just disappeared from my life without my registering the reality of his death. I never said goodbye to him. Until tonight.

The Ninth Bull of Tao — Reaching the Source
Too many steps have been taken returning to the root and the source.
Better to have been blind and deaf from the beginning!
Dwelling in one's true abode, unconcerned with and without —
The river flows tranquilly on and the flowers are red.

AS PROMISED, I meet with Laxmi to tell her my decision. I have a ticket to Bangkok, and I will leave in a few days. There are many capable and willing followers who eagerly want to dedicate themselves to the high-tech future of this movement. I am grateful for what I have learned, but I cannot stay.

"Where do you live?" she asks.

"In Canada. In a city called Edmonton."

"Is there a Rajneesh centre there?"

"No. No centre."

"Good. Then there is something you will do for Bhagwan."

"What is that?" I respond.

She smiles, knowing that I feel badly for turning her down. "You will marry Sant," she says, "and he will come to Canada to be with you. Together you will open a centre. Is it a big city?"

"Is this Rajneesh's request?" I ask.

"My request is Rajneesh's request. We both know that marriage means nothing. It is only a formality. If the centre does not work out in your city, you can try somewhere else. Vancouver perhaps."

Has Sant been a part of this plan? Has our whole relationship been geared toward this contrivance? Our time together has been quiet; there has been no mention of Canada. I cannot imagine him there. With me. In Edmonton. Or Vancouver.

All I can say to Laxmi is, "I will talk to Sant."

Strangely he is not at the gate, nor is he with his friends. I rush to sign up for my last darshan and manage to get a reservation for the next night.

Rajneesh has told us that obedience is the greatest sin. Listen to your intelligence, and if something feels right, then do it. You know what is right and wrong. For you. Don't let anyone tell you otherwise.

Nobody knows where Sant is. I go to darshan without having talked to him. There are hundreds of people in the garden, wanting to be noticed by the Master. He doesn't pretend to recognize everyone or to remember all the names he has given to his sannyasins.

I go up with several others and end up sitting within inches of Laxmi. I have not been back to see her. She leans over and whispers something to Rajneesh and he looks straight at me.

"You are leaving us?" he asks me. I nod, smiling, feeling special that he acknowledges me. Ah, my ego — it is still here and still strong. I shudder, worried that he may ask me to marry Sant. I can't. I just can't. He smiles at me. Here it comes.

"Don't come back." He says this seriously. I wince. He sees this and chuckles, playfully. "Were you planning to come back?"

"No," I say truthfully. Never.

"Good," he says. "Then we agree. Take what you know and use it. Share it."

Now he talks to everyone. "In sharing, you will be fulfilled. Share your laugh, your love, your voice, your ideas, and expect nothing in return. Do it for the joy of doing it. Madly in love. Be in love with life. Hmm? Make your work, play. Enjoy it. Be in the moment and you will do your best work. If you are not in the moment, nothing much will happen. It will only be an exercise. But if you share the moment, everyone around you will join. Together you will dance and everyone will be fulfilled."

He directs his words to me. "You will do that?"

"I will," I say. "I will try to do that!"

The Tenth Bull of Tao — Return to Society
Barefooted and naked of breast, I mingle with the people of the world.
My clothes are ragged and dust-laden, and I am ever blissful.
I use no magic to extend my life;
Now, before me, the dead trees become alive.

Dear Mom,
I'm travelling now, heading to Thailand to meet Cheryl.
I didn't get to Karachi. Next time. You will hardly recognize
me — I wear soft silk and walk slow. I miss you. I have
questions to ask you — I realize I do not know much about
how it must have been for you in India. It certainly has
changed me. Namaste.
Love you, Anne

SANT IS AT THE GATE. He's talking to a couple of new women. He nods at me and I nod back. It was good to have been with him and that is enough. We haven't spoken since Laxmi told me to marry him. I don't think he even knew about it. I don't say goodbye. He doesn't know I'm leaving, but that doesn't matter. "Love is a state of Being, not a relationship."

Life feels fresh and I feel free. My burden of self-doubt and guilt has been lifted. I walk away from the ashram, with an easy swing in my step, calmness in my being. I will try to live up to my new name — Ma Deva Mugdha — in love with the Devil and the Divine and remind myself to do everything with awareness.

Perhaps I'll find Jyoti at the taxi stand in Bombay and buy a lovely blue salwar kameez for my mother. She'll get a kick out of that.

ROSSDALE HOME IN EDMONTON, 1976.
IMAGE COPYRIGHT ELEANOR LAZARE AND *BRANCHING OUT* MAGAZINE.

SHEET ON
THE WALL

Edmonton, 1976

I'VE MADE GREEN CURRIED CHICKEN with coconut milk, jasmine rice, green papaya salad with custard for dessert. I call upstairs. "Supper in ten. How many are eating?"

Two voices chime down, "Three. No, four ... two!"

"Two?" I am impatient but try to sound blasé about it. "We were going to talk, remember? We need to talk."

I'm an out-of-work freelance filmmaker, with no equipment or financing. I wear orange clothing and my friends call me Mugdha, which is the name I was given in India by an eccentric guru known as Rajneesh. Last summer, twice a week, a group of like-minded weirdoes would meet in my backyard to do the madness meditation, which involves screaming and dancing around to loud music, blindfolded. The neighbours tolerated this bizarre behaviour — and the steady stream of humanity moving in and out of the place, including those visiting in vans parked out front and others throwing their tents down in the empty lot next door.

I spend most weekends at a commune north of the city. Everything they say about the place is true. It's akin to a perpetual love-in and yes, we *do* gather to cook, make music, chant, and dance naked under the full moon. There's a huge garden we all plant and harvest, a barn divided into living spaces, and several funky cabins along the Sturgeon River. In the summer there are extra places to camp and horses for those who like to ride.

One could say that my life is chaotic, unpredictable, and I'm fine with that for now. There is no man in my life, though. I think of having a child on my own but, truth is, I can't afford a family.

Meanwhile, the biological clock ticks on as my twenties draw to a close.

The only steady guy in my life is Wilbur the Worm. I write and perform a radio show for CBC that broadcasts in Alberta, Saskatchewan, and the Northwest Territories, teaching elementary kids music. Wilbur is a squeaky-voiced character who co-hosts the show with me, Anne. He is me, of course, and together we bring in thirty-five dollars a week.

I own an old house in a sweet part of Edmonton — Rossdale — down in the valley on the banks of the North Saskatchewan River. It was built in 1904, when this neighbourhood was a small town with its own school and a few stores. Back then, the river was a main thoroughfare; the big paddleboats would have passed right by my front door. I share my home with three wild and wonderful women — Lorna and Linda, identical twins, and Sylvie, a French Canadian from Northern Alberta.

They descend from the second floor with two men trailing. "I guess we're five of us eating," says Lorna.

"It smells so good!" says a new guy with an air of entitle-ment. I've never seen him before. Maybe it's just his British accent that makes him seem arrogant. I admonish myself for finding fault, but where did he come from?

"And who might you be?" I ask, lightly.

"Me?" he looks surprised, "I'm Keith, the architect. I'm with her." He points to Linda. She shakes her head and points to her sister. "No, you're with her ... you're with Lorna. I'm Linda."

"Of course!" He can't tell them apart and attempts to laugh it off. Hungry, he sits down with a wink.

The other guy, Michael, fills his bowl and leaves the room. "Have a good talk!" He is visiting from Montréal and pretty much stays out of everything, but Keith enthusiastically digs into the food.

"What's up? What do we need to talk about?" Linda asks.

"Well. Taxes are due. Mortgage rates just went up half a point." I try to present the bad news gently. "So I need to raise your rent by twenty dollars each."

"From ninety to one hundred and ten? For a room? That's a lot," Keith reacts. I stare at Keith in disbelief. How does he know how much they pay? He shrugs. "It is just my opinion. Pardon me."

"What an idiot!" I think to myself. It's a bargain for them, especially considering the "guests" who rarely contribute.

I just finished editing someone else's film and the pay was reasonable, but with all the extra costs around here, I'm counting every penny. I could find another editing job, but I'm anxious to make a film of my own.

Sylvie breaks the silence. "I think it's cool, no problem for me."

Linda just got back from travelling, so I know she's pondering whether or not she's even going to stay here. "There's a sort of room in the basement and a bathroom. Why don't we get another person?"

"What?" I cut her off, "Nobody wants to live in that pit. There's hardly any room and that old furnace is filthy, often smells like coal!"

Downing his food, Keith helps himself to more curry. "I should take a look ... I'm looking for a spot. In fact ... I could make this house into something really special ... that porch should be closed in — the heat is just pouring out of this place...."

I don't want to live with him! Just as I am about to be rude, the phone rings and I scramble to get it.

"Hello?"

"Hey, Wheeler!"

"Taylor!" I immediately recognize the drawl. He always talks like a cowboy and loves country music, but he's a city boy and lives in Vancouver where he runs the National Film Board studio.

"How are you, Wheeler? Haven't heard from you for a long time!"

I stretch the coiled cord down the hall so I can sit on the steps — away from the chatter. Keith is still going on and on. In fact, he's leading a parade down to the basement now. Oy-yoy-yoy!

"Well," I continue, "you haven't heard from me cause I've been travelling. I was in the East ... mostly in India ... I call myself Mugdha now."

He guffaws, "Oh ya. Someone told me that. Still happening, eh? Don't expect me to call you Moo-cow or whatever the hell it is ... what are you doing with yourself these days? Meditating?"

"Ya ... sometimes. But, I'm — you know — I'm working. I'm very busy." It's the truth — I'm busy shovelling the sidewalks, putting plastic over the windows, and trying to sustain some sense of "godliness" in my life. I'm thinking I might go back to being a music teacher.

"Busy, eh? Oh ya." He can see right through me. "Well, here's the deal ... I am sending five or six filmmakers out to places in the West that have not been documented in any way by the National Film Board. We don't get our share of the federal tax dollar out here, to tell our own stories, so I'm going to fight for this ... we need filmmakers like you and Radford. We need to tell stories that will illuminate just who we are."

Is he putting me on here? It sounds too perfect to be true. "You are speaking to the converted here, Taylor. We singing the same mantra —"

"Ya sure ... whatever that is. Come on, Wheeler. I'm being serious now."

"I'm serious too. You're right — we have our own stories to tell. Alberta contributes substantially to the federal tax pool — we should get our fair share of it out here."

"Exactly. But here's the thing ... I can only cover the expenses. That's all. If you come up with a good idea, then we'll present it to the national committee in April, and if they like it, then great. I'm fighting for a bigger budget next year so we can make three or four short films, and you will be in the running. No guarantees, of course."

I think I understand. "So you'll pay for gas, the hotels, and a per diem, so that I can scout out some stories, and then write them up with the hope that you and the guys in Montréal will like them?"

"Well, ya, you could put it that way ... that's the idea."

"I just have to invest my time?"

"You got it. But if you're too busy ..." I can hear him smirking. "I thought it would get you back into the real world here. You should be making movies, Wheeler, get back at it!"

It would take a couple of months out of my life but he's trying to make it happen out here when no one else is. If he's got Tom and others to play along, what's to lose? We're all on the same team.

"Okay. I'll do it. Where are you going to send me?"

"Northern BC — Prince George, Williams Lake — along the mighty Fraser River. Ever been up there?"

"Ah no." Very few people I know have been "up there," or want to be in the winter. "It could be interesting...."

"It could be fantastic!" He's hard-selling me now.

"When do you want me to go?"

"I have to spend this money in the next two weeks."

"Really! I mean.... So it's year-end money, I'm guessing." I know how the government works. If he doesn't spend his allotted dollars by April 1st, he'll have to send the unspent dollars back, and that could affect how much he gets next year. It's a crazy system!

"Exactly," he admits. "I thought, well, why not spend what we have and plan for the future, get some ideas brewing? Be ready to roll camera as soon as the new money comes in."

It's a good idea, very smart. "Okay. Sure. I'll go day after tomorrow. But I'll have to rent a car. Mine won't make it."

"Oh. Damn. Really?"

"Really. It's frozen up like a block of ice."

"Well, I'll have to cut the time down to —" He does the math. "— ten days. I can give you ten days of expenses."

"That's really only eight days, with two days of travel," I argue.

"Sorry, Wheeler. That's all I got. My office will call you in the morning. They'll send you some reimbursement forms to use. Fill them out when you get back. Save your receipts, eh?"

"Yes, of course." I have some questions, but he's in a hurry.

"This is good, Wheeler ... this is really good. Take lots of pictures."

And he hangs up!

Why Taylor thinks I have money on hand to rent a car and tour around for ten days taking pictures, I don't know, but my housemates manage to cough up their rent in advance and, gulp, Keith moves in downstairs, paying enough to cover the utilities. You don't always get what you want.

I go to the Army and Navy Store and buy some long woollen underwear, then go rent a small truck. I am stoked with the possibility of making my own little movie, even if the odds are not in my favour. I wonder who else he is sending out there. Who is my competition? No matter. After several months of hibernating in my metaphorical cave, it's time for me to re-enter the marketplace.

It takes a long day to drive the five hundred miles on a two-lane highway over the Rocky Mountains into the heart of British Columbia. With my heater turned up full, I cruise into Prince George, or PG as the locals call it, and find a motel. This is a pulp and paper town and can smell like rotten eggs. Tonight, it's in a dead fog. I can hear music playing at the pub across the highway from my new digs.

This is extraordinary luck. A hip new band, Chilliwack, is touring the North and they are terrific. If I had a film camera with me I'd shoot them right now, because they'd be a great hook for any film about the North. But they won't be back in the near future, so realistically that idea is just pie in the sky. But they do provide me with an opportunity to dance and party with a wild group of hard-working people, and to get personal over a couple of drinks.

Working at the pulp and paper mills at forty below sounds really tough, but obviously it pays well, and when they have time off, these people like to live it up. I am surprised to see so many East Indians in the crowd — that peaks my curiosity.

One guy with a few drinks under his rodeo belt buckle tells me, "Oh ya ... there are lots of them Pakis up here. They work at the mill. Takin' the jobs, eh? I don't know what kinda deals they're makin' — but people are none too happy about it, I can tell you that!"

I ask the big woman behind the bar, "Are there a lot of ranches up this way? Beef cattle? Farms? Anything besides lumber?"

"Oh ya," she says. "We got everything. A real variety of folks. There's a new community college, just opened. I'm taking a heavy equipment course; going to move to Fort McMurray."

"Oh ya! I've been there," I tell her, trying to sound tough — like her — hoping she'll open up to me. "Are there many women drivin' heavy equipment these days? I mean, that's pretty impressive."

She looks at me sideways. "Ya, a few. Why do you ask?"

Does she think I'm coming on to her? Or maybe I sound like an idiot, putting on the tough babe thing. I'll just be honest.

"I'm just interested. I'm looking for ideas. I'm working for the National Film Board. They make documentary films, and they've sent me here to see what's happening. I'm mostly interested in stories about women and what they do up here."

She nods, wondering if I'm for real of not. It does sound far-fetched. "There's a shelter for battered women, you know. It opened a couple months ago. That's where you'll find some stories about what it's like for women up here."

"Thanks! Wow. That's amazing. There are not many shelters around, even in the big cities. I will check that out. Thanks."

"Good!" she says, sincerely. "About time someone from the outside took an interest." She writes down the address by heart, so clearly she is connected in some way, though she does not look like she needs a place of refuge.

The shelter is run by a circle of churchwomen who have secured a humble house that is full right now, with two families. They welcome me warmly and introduce me to a mother with two children, who tells me that her husband lost his job at the mill and took it out on her. "I was afraid for my kids ... he beat me up ... a bunch of times ... and my boy was starting to challenge him."

"Why did he lose his job? Can you tell me?"

Her answer is quick. "He was lazy. Drank too much. Wasn't worth his wage ... a slacker. His dad and his uncles all worked at the mill — he thought it was his birthright."

"Did the loss of his job have anything to do with the East Indians who have moved up here?"

She smiles. Something about the question amuses her. "Oh yes, it has a lot to do with that. Those Indians ... they work hard and long, eh? They never complain. Some of them are moving up into management, too. That really bugged him." She almost laughs out loud. "He didn't like working for them."

"I guess!" I murmur. "But if they were worth more as employees...."

"Yup. Exactly. He was such an idiot. Still is." She shifts in mood, getting suddenly serious. "Their women, the ones that are brought in from India, have it hard, eh?"

"Really?" I say, probing, like I've never met an Indian woman. "How's that?"

She looks around to see if anyone is listening. "Well, last week, one of them came here. She was so beautiful. She had a daughter. A baby. And she was pregnant with a second. I don't know how she heard of this place, but she did, and she came here, wanting to get away from her husband, who beat on her all the time. She wanted to go home to India."

"Oh my God! She was taking a big risk! Was it an arranged marriage?"

"Yes!" She looks amazed. "Can you believe it? She had never met him until she arrived in PG, and right away they were married. Two years later, she's here, looking for help. Desperate. I cried for her."

"What happened to her? Where is she now?" I ask.

"It was intense. The husband came looking for her, but they —" she refers to the older women who run the place, — "wouldn't let him in. They were awesome. Strong — calm.... The guy was outside yelling for his wife to come out. But the woman just stayed out of sight. We didn't know what he was saying, of course, but she was terrified. Then more Indian men came and they tried to take him away, but he refused. Then more men came, and it got scary. A couple of the older women here went outside but the men wouldn't talk to them, told them it was not their business. They wanted to take this poor young woman away. I think she was maybe eighteen years old. At the most."

"What a scene," I mutter. "She was afraid for her life, I bet."

"Ya. Then some other women drove up in a big truck ... they were from the college. I think they volunteer here sometimes ... and they were brave ... they didn't take any shit from these guys."

"Was one of them ... a big girl covered with tattoos?" I ask.

"Winnie, ya. She's something. She's going to drive one of them big trucks. Have you seen them — monster trucks they use to build dams and like that? She was ready to fight — she has arms like ... huge."

"Ya ... I know. I met her. So then?"

"Wouldn't you know?" she shakes her head, disgusted, disappointed, "The holy-moly men got together and worked things out. That's the way it is, eh?"

"What happened exactly?"

"A minister, I don't know what church he was from but you know, he had a collar on, right? Christian minister, old guy — and a what? Hindu priest? Wore a turban — came in here and talked it over and worked things out."

"What do you mean, 'worked things out?'"

"Well, the husband was allowed in, and he was ... like you know ... sorry. He said he was sorry. I know she didn't believe him. But ... what could she do?"

"She went back?!" I am appalled. "She went back to him, after this ... big scene...?! He would have been outraged, humiliated —"

"She said he'd kill her."

We look at each other. Thinking. What can one do in such a situation? "The women here go and visit her twice a week," she offers. "They are not going to let anything really bad happen to her."

"Good ... that's good," I stutter, "but —"

"I know," she concurs.

What a story, I think, but a hard one to document. I spend a couple of days talking to different women, writing down the facts and contacts for future reference. In two or three months, though, this situation will be different — it is impossible to predict. But it's on my list because more stories will emerge, some of them similar. This little city is an unexpected vortex where east meets west.

I give Prince George three days, and then move on with only five days left to come up with something I can pitch with confidence.

I follow the Fraser River, which snakes its way south like a dazzling ribbon of fresh snow. There is little traffic on the highway, mostly huge trucks. The vast expanses of frozen wilderness make me revere the people who survived here before the world discovered its riches.

I pull in at Quesnel for gas and have an early lunch. Several 18-wheelers are clustered around a small café. Chances are good that this is the best place on the highway to eat.

I sit at the counter between two smokers wearing cowboy hats. They acknowledge me politely, glancing briefly at my attire. I'm wearing a long orange cape, with an orange Tibetan wool cap, fully aware that I am surrounded by men in blue jeans and ski jackets.

"What's good here?" I ask the man to my right.

He's friendly. "Chili con carne, if you're driving by yourself."

He laughs. So does the guy beside him. "Otherwise, I'd order the double-Denver."

By the time I finish my bowl of chili, we're good buddies, and I've discovered he's Shuswap from Williams Lake. He knows everyone in this neck of the woods. "I'm looking for stories," I explain to him, "stories that people in Vancouver, or Toronto, would not have heard. Stories about this part of the country."

"I don't give a damn about the people in Vancouver or Toronto, but if you want a good story, go see Augusta Evans. I don't know where she is this winter, but my auntie will know."

He draws an intricate map on a napkin so I can find his auntie, who lives in Soda Creek, which is a reserve. "She lives down river from the old mission," he explains.

I thank him for the tip and promise to say hello from him. He suddenly tears up. "Augusta knew my great-grandmother, eh? She is one of the old ones. She can still speak the language and knows everyone. Say hi from Tommy for me."

I drive into Soda Creek and easily find Aunt Edna. She doesn't question my intentions and tells me a little about Augusta. "Yes, well, she's going to be ninety years old next fall or maybe she is already! She was the daughter of the chief and the smartest girl in class. Ya. She is older than me, but she is like my sister. Ya. And she plays the harmonica, knows all kinds of songs, eh? Ask her to sing for you!"

She draws me another map. This one leads me deeper into the wild, following a narrow road that climbs up through the forest to a plateau. The road has recently been cleared, and a snowplow is parked close to an old abandoned hall. I pull in beside it and get out to walk over to the lip of the gorge. From here, I can look down over the forest and see the river that has always been the source of life for the Indigenous people. The valley looks beautiful, untouched by modern highways and industry. It is so quiet and still up here; I feel alone on the planet.

Grabbing my camera and my purse, I lock up, though I have not seen anyone since I left Edna's. I find the path beyond the hall where the clearing narrows into a white line that disappears into the trees. The surface of light snow remains unbroken by footsteps. No one has walked here for weeks, maybe months.

The snow is two- or three-feet deep in places, with a hard crust of ice hiding beneath the surface. I take a couple of falls and learn to go slow. Edna remembered coming here with her father when she was a little girl. They used the cabin Augusta is in this winter for hunting.

I cross several clearings where the snow has drifted into dunes. Plunging through them, I get wet right up to my chest. I stop occasionally to brush myself off and look around. The angle of the light shining through the trees in long shafts reminds me that the day is short and it will be dark soon. It feels like a cathedral in this old forest, sanctified and wondrous, but I don't want to be here alone when the lights go out.

It intrigues me that this ancient woman has chosen to live out her last days alone, with no electricity, no well, no phone, and clearly no visitors.

By the time I see the little shack nestled perfectly beneath the cedars, I am weak in the knees. There is no apparent smoke coming out of the chimney, no footprints around the place. Temperatures can plummet from ten above to fifty below overnight, and I can already feel the change happening. She must make her own fires, cook her own food. Heaven help her if she has an accident. Perhaps she's not here at all. Perhaps she's sick or, worse yet, dead!

The door has not been opened recently and is held shut by the hard-packed snow. I stop and listen, but hear nothing. Even the chickadees have fallen silent as I stand there, readying myself for whatever I might find.

I knock on the door and wait. Hearing nothing, I start to dig away at the snow with my hands.

Then I hear a shuffle of footsteps, a bang and a slam, and I realize that someone is pushing against the closed door from inside. Between the two of us, we pry it open enough for Augusta to peek out at me and smile.

"Hello! Have you come for coffee?" She says this with such warmth and delight, I feel like an old friend who was expected.

"Of course! Coffee would be wonderful!"

The humble interior is neat and swept, and surprisingly warm. Pop bottles and plastic containers are cleaned and stacked on makeshift shelves along the walls. She masterfully throws a lump of coal onto the fire that glows smokelessly in her open stove. A line of hand-rolled cigarettes lies neatly on her cedar plank table beside a small transistor radio — the one extravagance in the place.

Ladling water into an enamelled coffee pot, now black with use, she asks my name and how I managed to find her hiding place. I tell her hello from Edna and Tommy, whom I met at the station, and she is pleased. "Ah!" she exclaims. "That boy was a rascal — I delivered that boy ... and his two sisters, ya...."

"Really?" I exclaim. No wonder he wept when he spoke of her.

"Ya, I watched him grow up. He has a job?"

"I think so — he was driving a big truck."

That pleases her. Humming, she opens a cupboard and pulls out some soda biscuits and a jar of peanut butter. Chuckling, she admits, "I love peanut butter!"

So do I, which is good, because it may be all she has to eat. I pull out an Eat-More chocolate bar from my bag, and she lights up. "I love those!"

It doesn't seem to matter that I am blonde, young, and a stranger. She talks to me like I am her granddaughter, her confidante, her best friend, or her neighbour. When the coffee is poured, she automatically starts to tell her stories, as she has done, it seems, countless times. Each one has been crafted with the telling, starting simply, drawing you in, and ending with a strong conclusion. Every story leaves you wanting another story.

"I was born in the forest. Ya. Near here. The forest provided everything for my people. I will show you sometime — in the spring is best. We would gather everything we needed — food, medicine, moss. We did everything together. We ate together, slept together, had babies, died ... all together."

Every once in a while, she stops and pulls out her harmonica to play a tune. "Do you know this one?" she asks with a twinkle in her eye, then starts to sing. Some are songs from school, and others hinge on the blues. I know most of them and add a little percussion, drumming on the table, adding a harmony, which pleases her.

By four o'clock, it's dark; there is no question that I'm here for the night. She hands me a blanket. "I will tell you the story of the first men who came for gold — they were lost. My grandfather found them and brought them to our place near here. They stayed the winter. Ya. And in the spring, my uncles went with them, hunted for them, provided them with meat. Ya. My uncles showed them the way to the shining waters where they 'found' gold. That's what they said, 'Found!' Like we didn't know it was there. Of course, we knew it was there! It was beautiful.

"Then more men came; our people traded with them. Year after year, they would come looking. We'd tell them how to live here in the forest, sharing everything. Most of them didn't stay long."

"Did they thank you?" I ask.

"No, they did not thank us." She laughs — what a joke. "They only wished it was easier and warmer. Some of them complained, oh ya, especially if they had to stay the whole winter. Many of our women had children from these men. Like my auntie. She thought the man would stay, but he left in the spring as soon as he could. Never came back. No."

"And the baby?" I ask. "What became of the baby?"

"Oh," she says, without any judgement, "she was a strong girl, a good girl. We all loved her."

"We lived under the ground in the winter, ya. We'd dig down and make a big round room, with a place for the fire in the centre. Then we made a roof with wood and hides. Against the wall, we put a big tree trunk that was cut like stairs so we could go up and down. That was our home in the wintertime, ya. These were big places — sometimes ten, fifteen, twenty people would live there."

I can imagine the trappers or gold-seekers, clutching their bounty, hunkered down amongst these people, cooped up for months, crazy to leave.

"Before the gold diggers, the men came for fur, and my father was happy to trade them for blankets, guns, and alcohol. But soon there was trouble, sickness, and fights."

She likes that I want to know more. "I had three children, ya. Three from my own body. And ten more were given to me. Ten. Of thirteen children, only one is alive. And all but one died of alcohol. I don't drink. I never drank. No. I knew what it would do to me."

This truth brings tears to her eyes. "Only one boy wanted to learn — the stories, the plants in the forest, the food, the chants — the only one who wanted to know how to smoke the fish and make the medicines. He was given to me when I was sixty-nine years old. He died. He had an accident."

That is as much as she can say about him, for now. She mourns as she has done a thousand times, sitting alone at this table, smoking and remembering. Tears roll down her wrinkled face and she stays silent, thinking about her loss.

She insists that I sleep on the cot, but I refuse. We pull the mattress off the bedframe and make two comfortable beds. She has a spare toothbrush that she found in a ditch when she was walking to town. It's still new in its plastic package. She gives it to me proudly. Finally someone who will appreciate it! A nun taught her to brush her teeth and she still has most of her own. "It is why I have lived so long," she declares. "I can eat anything!"

The place is warm and dark as we crawl under our blankets, fully clothed. She continues to tell story after story, each one presented like a precious gift.

In the morning, we have more crackers with peanut butter, and she pulls out a special jar of jam she has been saving.

"I wish to tell you the story of my mother. Her father fought with Louis Riel. Do you know that name?"

"Yes, he was the much-loved leader of the Métis."

"Good." Impressed that I know this, she continues, "They

lost their farms and had no place to go, so they wandered west and north. My mother's family came here ... they didn't want to come, no, but they lost the rebellion. And she married the Chief — my father was the Chief. She had to learn to live in the forest. Everything, so different. When I was four I was sent to the school, at the mission. I stayed there for nine years. Then I went to live with my grandmother until I met George Evans. His mother was Shuswap but his father was Welsh. So he had no status. We couldn't live on the reserve. We didn't belong. George didn't know what he was, half Welsh, half Indian. He drank too much, but he was good with horses. He got a job on a ranch, and I did too. I cooked, cleaned, did the laundry. It was lots of work. Long days. They gave us a one-room cabin to live in."

In the morning, Augusta and I go outside and gather some wood — there's lots of it under the snow. Though she's fit and willing, the logs are heavy, and I can see that she must struggle to keep her cabin heated. There is no hint of self-pity or concern about what might happen to her in the future when she cannot do the work. For now, she rummages down into the heap, digging to where the wood and coal has stayed dry. "Here's a good one!" She shows me a big log. "It's dry and cracked, and the bark is falling away."

"Where do you live?" she asks.

"Alberta. East of here, over the mountains ... on the flatlands."

"Oh, I see." This makes sense to her and she sings, "Oh give me a home, where the buffalo roam...."

I sing along. "And the deer and the antelope play." We giggle — and harmonize to the end. "Where seldom is heard, a discouraging word, and the skies are not cloudy all day."

"That's how it is for sure," I say, "but the buffalo don't roam anymore."

"No," she admits, "they are gone. That was a long time ago. In the old days, we traded fish and berries for buffalo."

I avoid saying much about myself. My life is void of adversity or privation. What is there to say? She has lived through so much and has emerged with such dignity and purpose. She delights in telling me what she has learned.

"We used to trade with the men who built the railroad. They came from Alberta. When I was a young woman, my family walked to the place where they were working — near Jasper. It was a big camp."

"That's far away! Hundreds of miles!" I am amazed.

"Ya, it was a long walk. But I was young and excited to see somewhere new. There was a man," she says, disappearing into her memory for a moment, "who cooked for the others. He had long, thick, black hair tied back. There were others like him, but he was the one who wanted our food. He was willing to trade. We brought him wild vegetables he'd never seen. And berries, he loved the berries. He welcomed us and gave us tea. At first, we thought he was from a distant tribe, and I thought he was a good-looking man." She grins mischievously, like the young girl she was. "I liked him, and he liked me."

I can imagine the flirtation during the berry exchange.

"But then he told me that he was from China. Ya. From beyond the sunset. Across a great water. He could not come with us. He had family. A big family, and he missed them. But he looked like us. He laughed like us. Ya." She smiles, still holding the prize wood in her arms. "I couldn't go with him. My father would not let me go with him. My father was strong, and strict."

"Yes." I can relate. "Mine was too."

"What did he do?" she asks.

"He was a doctor."

"A doctor?" she asks.

I nod proudly. "Apparently he wanted to be a doctor from the time he was a young man."

"Ah. He had a calling."

"I guess. He was a good doctor — he and my mother met when they were children."

"That's a nice story. I have never been to one of your doctors. I don't like the idea of it. Cutting pieces out. I want to die with all my parts still together!" She chuckles at the thought. "I'm old-fashioned, I guess. I'm lucky to live so long."

I stay a second night, giving us time to stack up a good amount of wood and coal next to her stove. I worry that she's low on food, but she insists that she has enough. Her niece will come next week on a snowmobile with everything she likes.

Clasping my hands in hers, she sends me on my way. Whether or not I make this film, I will visit her in the spring and share the pictures I have taken.

I RETURN HOME to a household in transition. Sylvie is moving out. Lorna and Linda have determined they don't want to live with each other anymore. I decide to paint the house in case I need to sell it soon.

After months of writing and rewriting proposals, and endless committee meetings and telephone debates, Taylor calls me to tell me the good news. "Augusta" has been pro-grammed; we have been given the green light.

The bad news is that I only have four days to shoot it, with a three-person crew. I'd better know what I want and how I am going to get it, because the money is finite.

This is my first solo flight as a filmmaker. Up to now, I have worked within a group of guys, who'd been at it longer than me and knew things I didn't. I relied on them. I'd never gone to film school; neither had they. We figured it out as we went along. The crew on this show are all film school graduates, I think — talented professionals. I don't know them at all but will have to take the lead. There will be no one to blame but myself if I fail.

Six months after meeting Augusta, I return to Williams Lake ahead of the others to discover that Augusta is not at her cabin. She is living in a shack beside the highway, close to her only surviving son and his family. She's happy to see me and anxious to show me around. "I thought you'd never come back!" she laughs.

"Oh, I'm sorry, I didn't know how to get in touch with you. I have three friends who want to meet you too. We want to put your stories on film."

"Oh ya? You want to hear my stories again? And again?" She chuckles.

I have decided not to direct anything, to just trust my instincts. It will be more authentic if I just let her do whatever she does, and follow her without interfering. I'll stay as much out of the way with the crew as I can, and just watch. She wants to go see her friend, Edna, so that's what we'll do first.

Augusta and Edna are two of the few among their people who still speak Shuswap. Every summer, they smoke salmon together in the old way, in a lodge by the river, close to where Augusta's boy drowned. "He was given to me by a niece — and we used to walk everywhere, all over is valley together. I taught him everything I knew. I took care of him, then he took care of me, you see. But he went fishing. None of his friends wanted to go with him, so he went alone. Ya. No one should fish alone, but he couldn't find anybody to go with him that day. And he fell in. Ya. He fell in, I guess, and the river took him. That was the last I saw of my boy. Ya. I never saw him again."

She goes to the reserve whenever she can, so that she can visit the graveyard where some of her children, the ones who have status, are buried, including this boy.

Dozens of wooden crosses, which were once painted white and planted in neat rows, are now rotting and leaning awkwardly, this way and that.

"That's not the way we used to bury our people," she explains, "but after the sisters came, everything changed, ya. My people were put in the ground, in boxes, up there, in rows. We were forest people; we left our people in the forest."

Using her walking stick as she walks up the hill, she talks to herself, to her loved ones long gone. The crew and I wait at the bottom of the hill outside the dilapidated fence that surrounds the cemetery, so she can have her time alone.

My soundman, Ralph, has a quizzical look on his face. I have forgotten that she is wearing a new invention — a wireless microphone, which allows us to record her from a distance. He hands me his headphones so I can listen. Her voice is so present. I hear her muttering to herself as she moves through the overgrown grass and wild flowers.

"Hello, my people, Augusta has come to be with you. It's been a long time, but I had no one to drive me." She snaps off some wild daisies as she heads toward a broken marble headstone, the top lying awkwardly on the ground. "Oh no, what has happened here? How did this happen? My boy? Who did this?"

This is one of the few stone markers in the yard. I ask Ron, the cameraman, to zoom in on her with our long lens as she struggles to upright the broken piece. I want to rush up and help her, but the act is too personal, too intimate.

She continues to talk to her boy. "Your name is in two pieces — but I'll rest the top part here." With all of her strength, she raises the fallen marker and rests the bigger half upright against the base. "There you are, my dear boy. I'm going to put some fresh flowers here too — the ones you like. I'm sorry I haven't been up here lately. It's so far. Ya. But these people, I don't know who they are, drove me here. Ya. Nice people. They like my stories. They listen. I told them about you."

She cleans up around the stone, then stands and chants in Shuswap. Her voice is amazingly strong and we can hear her as it echoes through the valley.

"Mmm ... you always liked that one, ya?" she says to her boy.

If a Native man marries a non-Native woman, she gains legal Native status and reaps the benefits given to the treaty members by the Canadian government. There are women as white as I am, living here on the reserve who, along with their children, are eligible for free education, medical coverage, and other forms of assistance. Augusta, on the other hand, lives on a minimum old-age pension, which is less than a hundred dollars a month.

"At one time, I had eleven mouths to feed! Ya. All on welfare and some sewing I did, some work here and there. Most of the children were status but —" she stops for a moment, as though she can see them all "— but, we had a good time. I have no regrets."

At the age of five, she was sent to a Catholic residential school on the reserve. The building still stands in the valley, close to the church. "They taught me how to read and write, that was good. And how to plant seeds, ya, to grow my own food. I have always had a garden full of vegetables and berries. Different from the ones you find in the forest. Sweeter. I learned lots of good things from the sisters."

She still likes to go to church, mostly because of the music, but now she sings in Shuswap. "They didn't used to let us talk or sing in Shuswap. But I do it now. When I was just a child, I had to write on the blackboard, so many times, 'I will not speak Shuswap anymore.' Even though God knew this was unkind. He didn't care if I spoke Shuswap! The nuns just wanted to know what we were saying. They always thought we were doing something bad when we spoke our language. But God didn't care. God has more important things to worry about! And besides, he understands Shuswap. He was here before the nuns came; he was here long before that! He has always been here. He is not a person like the nuns said ... no ... he is much more than that. Not a man, not a woman. God is the spirit that gives life to all living things."

She takes us back to the forest, where she patiently describes how they once made good use of every living thing — the plants, the bugs, the bark, the fungi, and the animals they hunted, of course. Everything had a purpose. Some plants cure, while others kill, she tells us. Each is precious and each has its place. Everything depends on everything. Buddha could not have said it better, or lived with more awareness, I think to myself.

"This is the moss we use to pack the newborn baby. It is soft and keeps the skin dry. But this other moss is for dressing wounds. This willow will cure the headache, or sore joints. Chew on it, find a nice juicy branch, and suck out the bitter water. It will take away your pain and it will give you energy when you are tired. This berry we use to keep the meat from going bad. We pound it into the flesh, then dry it in the sun. It is very tasty and will last for months." She stops to snack on the salmon berries and gathers enough to fill the two discarded containers she rescued from the roadside, where we parked.

The next day, she dramatically waves down the bus on the highway, and we take it to town. She is very proud of her pension cheques from the government, and she has a stack of them. "I don't know where they come from or who decided that I should have them. Maybe it's because the government of Canada feels badly about what they did." She knows the driver and most of the passengers. Everything she sees out the window is special; it's as though this is the first time she has taken this ride. "Isn't this good?" she exclaims with delight. "Being carried everywhere. In the old days, when an old person could not walk very far, they stayed in one place and died."

The town of Williams Lake has a typical main street, with one of everything. She shuffles into the bank, oblivious that our camera is following her, and waits patiently for her turn. She opens the envelopes, one by one, and hands over the cheques. Carefully she signs them with perfect penmanship. "I must pay the rent tomorrow, for me and my son," she explains.

Thanking the teller for turning the cheques into money, she leaves. "My father signed a treaty with the government. Ya. He didn't think he got a very good deal from them. He'd never done anything like that before and he didn't get any money for it, as least, not that I know about. But they send me this money, every month. He would be surprised to know this."

We don't stay in town long. She has a short list of things to get before we head out — matches, tobacco, batteries for her radio, and some pumpkin seeds. "All the people here want is your money," she declares, as we march through a mall. And she's right.

"Do you ever worry about not having enough money?" I ask her.

She laughs. "I never had enough money. I am richer now than I ever was. Life was better when there was no money. When we lived in the forest, we loved one another. There was no stealing. No wastefulness. No drinking and getting mean. Sometimes we were cold, and sometimes people got sick — but as a child, I knew that I belonged and that made me strong."

As we walk back to her place from the bus crossing, along the ditch, she picks up more containers. "If we find enough glass bottles, I'll make a bottle piano for my grandchildren when we get home. You put different amounts of water in each one. It's a beautiful sound. You won't believe it, but these bottles can sing! The sisters taught us how to do that. Yes, they taught us lots of things."

Long ago, Augusta saw a woman die, giving birth to her baby. It was a shock to her. When her first baby was about to be born, she sent her husband to get the doctor. She gave him some money, but he didn't come home for days, so she went through the delivery alone. "I promised myself that I wasn't going to let another woman go through something like that, alone. No. Not if I could help it. And when my husband did show up, he was drunk," she tells me. "He said the doctor didn't come because he couldn't pay him. What kind of doctor is that? What kind of husband? He spent the money I saved, on drink! My husband died young, and I never got married again. Once is enough."

She bought a homesteading book and memorized the chapters on midwifery. And over the next fifty years, she went whenever she was called to deliver the babies, how many she doesn't know. Hundreds, maybe thousands. "And I never lost one of them ... no, I never lost one. And I never charged anyone. I know doctors charged, even when they lost the baby! Yes they did."

It feels wrong that I should be getting paid to make this movie. Here is Augusta, sharing everything with me while living in poverty, without running water or electricity. There must be a way to pay her.

The last thing we film, before leaving, is her playing the harmonica, and then her grandchildren (she is everyone's granny) come and have a singsong with her. She is totally consumed by their efforts to learn the words, and we drive away unnoticed.

Just a few days after I get back to Edmonton, I get a call from Taylor, raving about what he has seen. "But there's a problem, Wheeler. That day you shot in the forest — the footage is lost."

"What do you mean, lost?"

"Well, there was a light leak in the camera, not sure how it happened, something didn't seal right, I don't know ... so there's a wide white strip right down one side of the image. It's unusable."

"Well, then, let me re-shoot!"

"No, can't do that. There's no money left to do that."

"But, that was important, very important. That was footage that can never be replaced. Nobody else knows what she knows! It was priceless."

"Sorry. Listen, you have lots of great stuff here for a fifteen-minute movie, and you'll have trouble getting it down to that. She's terrific. You don't need it, trust me on this." I hammer away at him, but it's pointless. Augusta's forest is out of the picture. I feel a heavy sense of loss. If I could afford to go back myself and shoot it, I would.

I decide to cut the movie myself, mostly because I love watching her and listening to her, and I can put more money into other things, like music, which was budgeted pathetically low. We won't need much music. She often talks right to the camera, with such warmth and humour that the content holds the audience on its own.

It's autumn when the little movie is completely finished and ready for a showing. I take the first answer print from the laboratory in Vancouver and drive north to Williams Lake to show Augusta what we've done together.

I pick her up in my rental van and we head over to Edna's on the reserve, where there is electricity. While they have coffee in the kitchen and chatter away in Shuswap about I don't know what, I tack a white sheet up on Edna's living room wall and set up the 16-mm projector. I pull the drapes closed and turn off the lights.

"All right, you two," I call to them, "it's time to come and sit in here." They did not see what I was doing while they were talking, cherishing their time together. As they come into the darkness and see the projector, they are bewildered. Saying nothing, Augusta takes a chair, places it in front of the projector and sits down staring into the lens. I realize that she thinks the projector is another camera and we're going to shoot again. She's ready to tell me her stories one more time.

"Turn the chair around, Augusta. It's going to be up there."

She looks around, surprised, "Edna, why is your sheet on the wall?"

Edna is as perplexed as Augusta. They both think I'm daft.

"Both of you. Turn your chairs around. Get comfortable. Look at the sheet on the wall. I have a surprise for you." Amused, they reposition themselves, as I flip the switch on the projector and the reels start to turn.

It is the best screening of my life. The first shot comes up of Augusta sweeping her raw wooden floor; it starts on her feet and tilts up, as we hear the transistor radio giving the local weather and messages. "That's me! Edna, that's me on your sheet! And that's you, talking!" She not afraid or proud, just bedazzled, as though she is watching a bit of wizardry. There is a message from Edna to Augusta to catch the early bus to town — and now Augusta is flabbergasted, thinking that Edna is on the radio now, instead of right here beside her.

I realize that she has never seen a film before, and had no idea what we were doing when we were here shooting it. To her, we were a group of young people interested in her stories, and she was happy to share what she knew to be true, with us.

Completely in the moment, she talks to her other self on the sheet, cheering herself onward. We cut to the church and there she is sitting in a pew, wearing her best scarf. The organ begins. "All right Augusta, you sing in Shuswap! No one will stop you!" She sings the hymn in the living room with herself on the screen, loud and strong, but I have edited out a couple of verses and that trips her up momentarily. "Augusta, you missed two verses ... go back! You know all the words!"

Sitting here in Edna's living room she watches herself visit the graveyard, and weeps. She sees the headstone on the ground, and she mutters, "Who keeps pushing that over. I thought I fixed that ... here it is down again."

Beneath some scenes, there is the distant sound of a harmonica and she croons.

The film ends with her walking down an ancient path along the river with credits rolling. Amongst the crawl of names, it is noted that the composer is Augusta Evans. She doesn't notice that at all; she is still in a trance.

When the film runs out, she turns to me, wide-eyed, "That was like a dream, just like a dream! Where did it go?"

"It was wonderful," agrees Edna. "The smokehouse was beautiful." For a while, they don't say another word, holding themselves in, mulling over what they have just seen. I rewind the film, and then ask, "Would you like to see it again?"

"Again? We can see it again?" They are in disbelief. "It's not gone?"

We watch it a couple of times, and then Augusta realizes that all we need to make this happen is electricity! We pack it all up and she has me drive her all over the countryside, to show the movie to her family, her friends, and her priest, always introducing it the same way. "I have something to show you! We have put all my stories in this tin can, but we can take them out and put them on your wall. You will see!"

I give her the cheque for the music — the harmonica playing I have used throughout the film is the score. She doesn't understand at all, but signs the contract, grateful to have more money than she has ever seen in her life. We go to the bank to cash it and everyone there stays after work to watch the film.

"What am I going to do with all this money?" she asks me.

"You could get running water."

"I am moving to my cabin next week, for the winter. I don't want anyone making a mess out there. Digging up the ground."

"Well, what would you like?" I ask.

"A new gravestone for my boy. Could we get that?" she asks.

"Of course. Whatever you want."

She holds my hand. I will never forget the strength in her grip, as she looks at me with tears in her eyes. Her face is a maze of lines mapping out what it is to be human. When she laughs, her eyes well up and tears flow freely. She sparkles with love and wisdom, living out her life in a quiet, truthful way. I don't know if I have ever met a more enlightened soul. She's mindlessly compassionate, has no ego, is always in the now, completely truthful and spontaneous. She is a true teacher by example — a guru gone unnoticed, but that matters not at all to her.

"This is a good thing we did, Anne. These stories will live forever now, dancing on the wall, won't they?"

"Yes," I assure her. "Forever."

"Then I have done what I was supposed to do."

I nod. I understand her sense of accomplishment.

"Ya, I have done what I was supposed to do," she repeats, "and you, my friend, have just begun."

"What do you mean? I ask.

"Well, it's time to tell your own stories — of what you know."

"I don't know where to begin."

"Start with yourself. Tell the stories no one else can."

Augusta Evans died at the age of 90, in 1978. *Augusta* (NFB,1976) is available on the National Film Board website at: **www.nfb.ca/film/augusta/**

AUGUSTA EVANS OFF TO SEE HER MOVIE AT WILLIAMS LAKE, 1977.
ANNE WHEELER ARCHIVES.

Acknowledgements

Having grown up without television, I was blessed with a childhood where music and storytelling were at the hub of every family gathering. For that reason I must acknowledge the raconteurs of my youth: my aunt Ruth MacLennan, who specialized in family lore, and my godfather Tom Payne, who spent decades in the Far North in search of gold. Both of them knew how to spin a yarn, titillating us with the remarkable unknown and their personal and secret observations that would otherwise be lost.

So many others have encouraged me to write down my own tales of adventure in a style akin to my spoken presentations. In particular I give credit to Joy Coghill, Cheryl Malmo, Gail Carr, Charlene Roycht, Glynis Whiting, Linda Crossfield, Betsi Warland, Ali Liebert, and Tess Elsworthy who read my early attempts, critically responded, and gave me courage to move ahead. More recently, the members of my writing group in La Manzanilla have watched these stories change shape over the course of the last six years at readings and story slams — there is nothing like a listening audience to give you pure and honest feedback.

Set in my twenties, these stories acknowledge several individuals who challenged me and shared their knowledge and wisdom. They are the stars, the mentors I most cherish.

I will always be indebted to the people I worked with in the early years of my career, those at Filmwest Associates and the National Film Board of Canada, who taught me so much about crafting a narrative.

In the later stages of bringing this book together Donaleen Saul became my guide, my confidant, my "substantiating" editor, which meant she worked with me for many months, defining the intention of each story. Together we gathered up a bevy of beta readers (thank you all), and reacted to their comments before sending the manuscript off, hoping to secure a publisher.

Amazingly, NeWest Press — a publisher I have admired since its beginnings — responded and Eva Radford, a much-respected editor, was assigned to work with me, polishing the manuscript, reviewing every nuance, making sure the stories are clear and concise. It has been a gift.

And finally I thank my extended family, my sons, and especially my beloved husband, Luben Izov, who has kept me emotionally and technically on course throughout this process. He is always there behind the scenes, ready to support and make my dreams come true.

Alberta-born ANNE WHEELER earned degrees in mathematics and music, while performing in theatre whenever possible. Her first films were documentaries, but by the 1980s she was making Canadian features such as *Bye Bye Blues, The Diviners, Better than Chocolate*, and *Loyalties*, winning numerous national and international awards. A master storyteller, she has garnered seven honorary doctorates, an Order of Canada, and a Lifetime Achievement Award (being the first woman to do so) from the Directors Guild of Canada. She lives in White Rock, BC, and continues to write, direct, and mentor younger filmmakers.